ScrapBook secrets

Shortcuts & Solutions

every scrapbooker needs to know

kimber mcgray

MEMORY
MAKERS
BOOKS

CINCINNATI, OHIO

www.mycraftivity.com

Scrapbook Secrets. Copyright© 2009 by Kimber McGray. Manufactured in China. All rights reserved. It is permissible for the purchaser to make the projects contained herein and sell them at fairs, bazaars and craft shows. No other part of this book may be reproduced in any form or by any electronic or mechanical means including information storage and retrieval systems without permission in writing from the publisher, except by a reviewer, who may quote a brief passage in review. Published by Memory Makers Books, an imprint of F+W Media, Inc., 4700 East Galbraith Road, Cincinnati, Ohio 45236. (800) 289-0963. First edition.

13 12 11 10 09   5 4 3 2 1

Distributed in Canada by Fraser Direct
100 Armstrong Avenue
Georgetown, ON, Canada L7G 5S4
Tel: (905) 877-4411

Distributed in the U.K. and Europe by David & Charles
Brunel House, Newton Abbot, Devon, TQ12 4PU, England
Tel: (+44) 1626 323200, Fax: (+44) 1626 323319
E-mail: postmaster@davidandcharles.co.uk

Distributed in Australia by Capricorn Link
P.O. Box 704, S. Windsor, NSW 2756 Australia
Tel: (02) 4577-3555

Library of Congress Cataloging-in-Publication Data

McGray, Kimber.
  Scrapbook secrets : shortcuts and solutions every scrapbooker needs to know / Kimber McGray.
    p. cm.
  Includes index.
  ISBN 978-1-59963-034-2 (pbk. : alk. paper)
  1. Photograph albums. 2. Photographs--Conservation and restoration. 3. Scrapbooking. I. Title.
  TR501.M42 2009
  745.593--dc22
                              2008042827

www.fwmedia.com

Editor: Kristin Boys
Designer: Kelly O'Dell
Art Coordinator: Eileen Aber
Production Coordinator: Greg Nock
Photographer: Al Parrish
Stylist: Nora Martini

Cover Illustration Credits—
Two women: ©Heather McGrath
Title border: Ute Hiltenkamp
Images available at www.istockphoto.com

Metric Conversion Chart

to convert	to	multiply by
Inches	Centimeters	2.54
Centimeters	Inches	0.4
Feet	Centimeters	30.5
Centimeters	Feet	0.03
Yards	Meters	0.9
Meters	Yards	1.1
Sq. Inches	Sq. Centimeters	6.45
Sq. Centimeters	Sq. Inches	0.16
Sq. Feet	Sq. Meters	0.09
Sq. Meters	Sq. Feet	10.8
Sq. Yards	Sq. Meters	0.8
Sq. Meters	Sq. Yards	1.2
Pounds	Kilograms	0.45
Kilograms	Pounds	2.2
Ounces	Grams	28.3
Grams	Ounces	0.035

ABOUT THE AUTHOR

Kimber McGray has always been a crafter of some kind since she was a young child. She found her way into scrapbooking through a friend who pushed her for well over a year. Once she began to play with the papers and tools we all know and love, there was no turning back. She jumped in with two feet and has enjoyed every moment of it. Over the last three years, Kimber has been fortunate to have been published in all the major scrapbooking and card making publications. She was also inducted into the 2007 Creating Keepsakes Hall of Fame. Kimber finds time to create the pages that fill her albums when she's not making the memories with her husband and two children in her hometown of Carmel, Indiana.

ACKNOWLEDGMENTS

As I am sitting here writing, I am wishing that my husband, Bill, could be here with me. He is currently serving a tour in Iraq. He continually expresses his extreme confidence in me, which has allowed me to find the strength to complete this project even in his absence.

Writing this book has actually spurred more creative time for me and my children, Andrew and Laura. They have sat right next to me and played with my stamps and inks while I was trying to figure out how to do certain techniques. It is so refreshing to see my kids play, and know there are no mistakes in crafting and not to be afraid to try something new.

To my friends who have seen me through this whole process, I would never have considered pursuing a book idea without your help. Tara Tuck gave me the push to try for a proposal, and Sherry Steveson gave me the tools to get the proposal on paper and held my hand through the process. Kim Moreno and Summer Fullerton created at a drop of a hat for me when I needed "just one more project" to fill a spot in the book.

To my wonderful contributors, who not only contributed their secrets for me to use in the book, but the art that went along to support it. Without you guys, this book would have been half of what it is.

Finally, to the amazing people who put this book together. To Christine Doyle, thank you for giving me the chance and for listening to a few different proposals before settling on this one. I appreciate the open mind and willingness to work with me. To Eileen Aber, for your amazing ability to organize and keep me straight with paperwork. And finally to Kristin Boys, your patience and ease to work with made this project very enjoyable. You worked your magic wand in more than one instance to polish my work into this beautiful book.

Thank you all for your hard work on this project! I have enjoyed it more than I could have ever imagined.

Contents

CHAPTER ONE: BEST PRACTICES
Secrets of scrapbook basics

CHAPTER TWO: EASIER WAYS
Secrets to simpler scrapping

CHAPTER THREE: MAKING DO
Secrets for scrapping in a pinch

CHAPTER FOUR: WHO KNEW?!
Secrets that may surprise you

bubbly
good
time

Laura - July '07

Just a little
afternoon fun
learning how to
blow bubbles
can be very
tricky!

SecreTs RevealeD

In the few years that I have been scrapbooking, I've learned many different tips and tricks—secrets that have made my scrapping easier, more productive and more fun. At crops I would find myself watching how a fellow scrapper used a stamp or a punch and marveling at how such a simple technique had escaped me. I signed up for classes and rejoiced at learning how using basic tools the correct way made life easier. Even now, I hear scrapbook secrets I didn't know; there are always a few tips and tricks my students share with me.

I've learned a lot from other scrappers. But many of the techniques in this book, I've learned from my own mistakes or from trying to stretch my supplies. This book came from wanting to put all these little secrets together in one place—I just had to spill my guts! But you won't find any grand revelations that will make headlines. What you will find are 50 basic techniques that will make scrapbooking easier and your layouts more interesting. From simple secrets to more surprising techniques, this is your source for have-fun and get-it-done ideas.

Tools & Materials

Even if you know the greatest scrapping secret in the world, being without the right tools will always hold you back from scrapping effeciently. In addition to a pencil, quality journaling pen, and the right kind of adhesive, these tools are a must-have for me and a necessity for completing many of the secrets revealed.

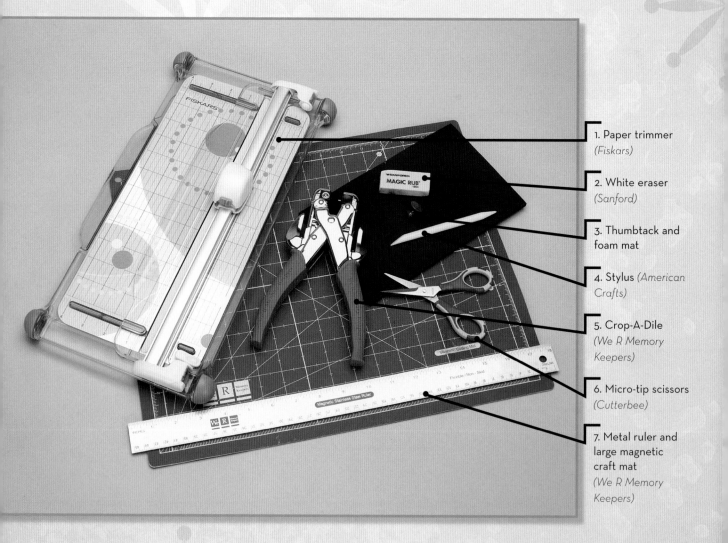

1. Paper trimmer
(Fiskars)

2. White eraser
(Sanford)

3. Thumbtack and
foam mat

4. Stylus (American
Crafts)

5. Crop-A-Dile
(We R Memory
Keepers)

6. Micro-tip scissors
(Cutterbee)

7. Metal ruler and
large magnetic
craft mat
(We R Memory
Keepers)

1. PAPER TRIMMER. A trimmer is a must-have for straight, precision paper cutting. A rotary trimmer is one of my favorites because you can switch out blades for different edges such as a scalloped edge.

2. WHITE ERASER. A white vinyl eraser will remove stray pencil marks easily and leave your paper clean. It won't smudge or discolor your paper when you use it.

3. THUMBTACK AND FOAM MAT. I prefer to use a thumbtack instead of a paper piercer, because it's easy to hold and make tiny pricks—and it's readily available. Use the thumbtack to make holes for all kinds of purposes like inserting tiny brads, marking measurements and hand-stitching. The foam makes it easy to punch the thumbtack right through paper.

4. STYLUS. A stylus is nice to have on hand. For me, it is the best thing for applying rub-ons. It can also be used to score paper when making cards.

5. CROP-A-DILE. This monster of a tool creates standard-sized holes in paper and card-stock, along with chipboard, fabric and thin metal with ease. It's also the handiest eyelet-setting tool around.

6. MICRO-TIP SCISSORS. These scissors have a short blade and come to a sharp point, making it easy to cut out patterned paper details and in between tight spaces on rub-on and sticker sheets.

7. METAL RULER AND MAGNETIC CRAFT MAT WITH GRID LINES. Because of its size—larger than 12" x 12" (30cm x 30cm) layouts—this dynamic duo helps you line up items nice and straight on your layouts.

Our Mermaid

Today we arrived at Fort Stevens the sun was shining so we headed down to explore the beach for a bit. Brad and Corinne sat down and buried each other's feet in the sand. Then they decided to make Corinne into a mermaid by forming her buried feet into the shape of a fin. Even Grant got into the act. They packed sand and formed her tail for about half an hour until it was just right. They added the scale detail and Corinne the mermaid was complete.

7/07 Fort Stevens, OR

Favorite Activities to do ON THE BEACH...

chapter 1

BesT PracticEs
SECRETS OF SCRAPBOOK BASICS

Scrapbooking is an art as well as an avenue for storytelling, so there are many different ways to create layouts. Among all the methods and techniques for pulling a page together, there are some essential basics to know—shortcuts that will help you scrap faster and better no matter what your style and method. Turn the page to get the best design secrets and helpful tool how-tos.

Pulling colors from your photos is the easiest way to make them pop.

all boy

This photo really captures you. You love to play outside and climb trees. As much as losing your tooth at 18 months due to a fall bothered me, today it just fits your personality! You are for sure ALL BOY!

Artwork by Kim Moreno

Whatever the purpose of scrapping, the focus is almost always a photo (or set of photos). So choosing patterned papers that complement a photo is paramount. The simplest way to build an attractive page around a photo is to pull the colors for your patterned paper from the colors in your photo. While Kim's son is wearing a red shirt, she pulls the main colors for her patterned paper, cardstock and embellishments from the background. The nice, neutral backdrop makes her son, in his red shirt, pop.

Supplies: Cardstock (WorldWin); patterned paper (Dream Street); chipboard letters (American Crafts); paper punch (EK Success); Misc: floss, ink, twigs, twine

AHA!

To conserve paper, cut out the center of the paper you plan on using for a photo mat.

Materials
focal photo
three patterned papers

1. Choose background paper
In the layout photo, brown, neutral shades appear along the perimeter, in the tree branch and hair. To re-create the look on a layout, add a brown patterned paper to the background to act as a border for the page.

2. Layer second paper
Most of the background in the photo consists of spotty green tones. To add a similar proportion of green to your layout, layer a large piece of green paper over the brown paper. Use a tone-on-tone pattern to mimic the mottled look of the photos.

3. Choose paper for details
Finally, you can see that there is a bit of light blue in the photo's background. To match that look, layer a small strip of blue paper over the top of the other patterned papers.

Another easy way to make your photos pop is to use the colors in them to choose complementary or contrasting colors for your paper. Here, Linda highlighted the blue in her photos (to highlight her son) using orange and green. Orange (which is opposite blue on the color wheel) contrasts with blue, while green (which is next to blue on the color wheel) complements blue, both of which make the color pop.

Supplies: Cardstock (WorldWin); chipboard accents, patterned paper, stamp (Inque Boutique); letter stickers (American Crafts); rub-on (Cosmo Cricket); buttons, ribbon (Making Memories); Misc: ink, paint

Artwork by Linda Harrison

Using the Rule of Thirds ensures a well-balanced layout.

One of the basic concepts in layout design is using the Rule of Thirds. The Rule of Thirds is a design principle that calls for dividing a layout into three visual sections either vertically or horizontally. Placing the most important pieces of your layout in each of these sections will ensure a viewer will not miss them and will also ensure a well-balanced layout. On this layout about my daughter, Laura, I divided my page into nine squares and used the Rule of Thirds to place my photos as well as the title, journaling and embellishments.

AHA!

At a loss for design ideas? You can scraplift your own layouts. There's no law against reusing great designs!

Supplies: Cardstock (WorldWin); die-cut tag, patterned paper (Pink Paislee); letter stickers (Reminisce); brads, chipboard shape, metal clips (Making Memories); acrylic flower (Heidi Swapp); Misc: ink

1. Divide layout

Start by dividing your layout visually into thirds, both horizontally and vertically. You should end up with three rows and three columns, creating a grid of nine squares.

2. Fill horizontal thirds

Place important elements in different horiztonal sections. For example, place your focal point, like the faces in my two main photos, in the top horizontal third. I placed the faces in my smaller photos in the middle horizontal third. I placed my journaling and patterned paper, secondary elements, in the bottom horizontal third.

3. Fill vertical thirds

Complete your layout by placing the title and embellishments in different vertical thirds. For example, I placed my title in the middle vertical third. I then placed small pink embellishments at the top of the left third and balanced those with additional pink embellishments in the bottom of the right third.

Materials

focal photo
additional photos
various elements (like embellishments and title letters)

There's no rule that says that the Rule of Thirds has to be followed in one, specific way. The thirds on my layout (on the previous page) are not so obvious. Plus, I divided my layout into both vertical and horizontal thirds. Summer, however, divided her layout very literally into three vertical sections. Placing a title two-thirds of the way down the page is another way in which Summer worked with the rule.

Supplies: Cardstock (WorldWin); patterned paper (EK Success, Heidi Grace); chipboard letters (Scenic Route); die-cut shapes (Cloud 9)

Secret [3]

A visual triangle keeps the eye moving around a page.

A visual triangle is a design principle that involves strategically placing elements at three points on a layout; when connected by invisible lines, the three elements create a triangle. The triangle draws the eye around the page. A visual triangle is a simple way to achieve balance and flow on a layout. There are different ways to implement a visual triangle; repeating the same color(s) is one way. Kim does this effortlessly in using three embellishments in pink and burgundy.

Supplies: Letter stickers, patterned paper, ribbon (Making Memories); stamps (Inque Boutique); Misc: ink, staples

Artwork by Kim Moreno

Place elements in a visual triangle of color

First, visualize a large triangle anywhere on your page. If you need help while you get the hang of it, draw the triangle on a transparency and place that over your layout. Then, simply place an element in the same color in each of the three corners. Using a visual triangle doesn't preclude adding that same color in a fourth spot—like the end of the burgundy ribbon, here—the triangle just ensures that at least three different places on a layout are covered.

Materials
3 elements in the same color

You don't have to stick with three embellishments to create a visual triangle of color. Here, I included the title as part of a visual triangle of royal blue—the title, plus the brads and the binder clip. As you can see, repeating a color that contrasts with the background of a layout really makes the triangle pop. I pulled the royal blue color from the color of the vase in my photo.

Supplies: Cardstock (WorldWin); patterned paper (Autumn Leaves, Scenic Route); chipboard letters (Heidi Swapp, Scenic Route); brads (Creative Impressions); ribbon (from flowers in photo); Misc: binder clip

Supplies: Cardstock (WorldWin); patterned paper (Glitz Design); letter stickers (American Crafts); brads (Creative Impressions); stamps (Hampton Arts); Misc: ink

Repeating the same type of element (such as a shape or a specific embellishment) is another way to successfully create a visual triangle. On this layout, Kim created a visual triangle by repeating the same embellishment on the page.

Artwork by Kim Moreno

Repeat the same shape

To create a visual triangle using three of the same elements, repeat the steps for creating a visual triangle of color (on page 17). Be sure to use elements in similar tones, like primary colors or pastel colors, to ensure that one element doesn't outshine the others.

Materials
three of the same element

Artwork by Sarah Hodgkinson

To create a visual triangle, you can forgo the single, large triangle in favor of creating smaller triangles of either the same color or same element. While the layout as a whole is not designed around a triangle, a grouping of three elements creates balance. Here, Sarah grouped similar elements into smaller triangles that she placed in opposite corners for symmetry. As you can see, using elements in slightly varying sizes adds a nice touch.

Supplies: Cardstock (WorldWin); buttons, patterned paper (Scenic Route); stamps (EK Success, Hampton Arts); Misc: ink, string

AHA!

For a no-fail design, group embellishments in odd numbers, like a group of five stars. The eye prefers odd-numbered groupings to even-numbered ones.

Materials

6 elements of either the same type or color

Create multiple small triangles

To create small visual triangles, follow the steps for creating a visual triangle of color (on page 17), only make the triangles much smaller, so that the elements are near each other or actually touching. You can place one, two or three smaller triangles on a layout.

Secret

[4]

The key to designing a great two-page layout is to think of the two pages as one big canvas.

Often the motivation for creating a two-page layout is to fit as many photos as possible on a page. It's easy to fall into the trap of placing the focal point photo on one page and then slapping additional photos on the other page where they will fit. The best thing to remember when working on a two-page layout is to think of it not as two separate pages, but as two halves of one big canvas. Let your photos, titles and design flow across both pages. Here, Summer's photos tell a story as they cross from the left page to the right.

Supplies: Cardstock (WorldWin); patterned paper (Karen Foster, My Mind's Eye); die-cut shapes (My Mind's Eye); chipboard letters and shapes (American Crafts, Pressed Petals); felt letters (American Crafts); buttons (SEI)

Artwork by Summer Fullerton

AHA!

You don't need to include extensive journaling on every layout. Sometimes the basics—who, what, when, where—are all you need.

4. Repeat additional elements

Repeat other elements, like the thin frame and the buttons, on both halves of the layout.

1. Choose a background

Start with the same background for both pages, like this bright white cardstock.

2. Place photos

Place a block of photos that spans the two-page spread. (See page 106 for the secret to placing a photo across a seam!)

3. Place design elements across spread

Start a single, large design element, like this diamond border made of patterned paper, on one half of the spread and continue it onto the other half.

Materials

two sheets of cardstock
photos
patterned paper
embellishments
pen
buttons

An easy way to successfully connect two halves of a design is to use background papers that are easy to seamlessly connect. Cardstock is a natural choice to repeat since there is no design to match up across a seam. Also consider using polka dots, stripes or small prints as I did here. Notice how the visual triangle formed by the title and two embellishment clusters (at the upper left and lower right) keeps the eye moving around the whole layout.

Supplies: Cardstock (WorldWin); patterned paper (Crate Paper); letter stickers (American Crafts, Scenic Route); chipboard swirls (Fancy Pants); brads, rub-ons, snowflakes (Imaginisce); bookplate (BasicGrey); Misc: corner rounder, embossing powder, ink

Secret

[5]

Tired of crooked borders? You *can* cut a straight decorative edge.

The quickest way to add a decorative border to a page is with decorative-edge scissors. Whether decorative scissors are new to you or if you have had them in your stash for years, the toughest part of using them is making a straight cut. Stay on course with an easy technique using a ruler and pen. While my daughter looked a bit "ungirlie" this morning by waking up with a bad case of bed head, I softened the overall page by adding scalloped-edge borders cut with my decorative-edge scissors.

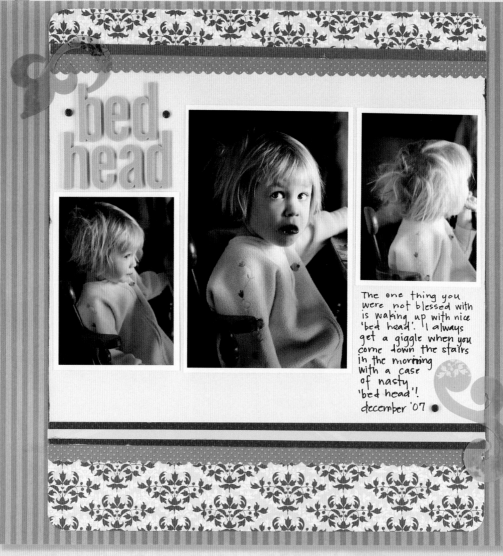

bed head

The one thing you were not blessed with is waking up with nice 'bed head'. I always get a giggle when you come down the stairs in the morning with a case of nasty 'bed head'!

december '07

Supplies: Cardstock (WorldWin); brads, patterned paper, swirls (Making Memories); decorative scissors (Fiskars)

1. Draw line with straightedge

Flip your paper over, and, using a straightedge, draw a line where you want your decorative edge to be. If you draw on the back side, there's no need to erase your marks later.

2. Cut along line

Flip your paper so that the portion where you want the decorative edge (and not the leftover portion) is on the left side of your scissors (if you're right-handed). Line up the bottom edge of the scissors with the line to make your first cut. Be sure to continue lining up the bottom edge as you cut along the remainder of the line.

Materials

paper
straightedge
pen or pencil
decorative-edge scissors

Even in short sections, hand-cut decorative edges can get a little wacky. Use your new-found technique to create perfect edges for beautiful cards.

Supplies: Cardstock (WorldWin); patterned paper (BoBunny, Making Memories); stamp (Hero Arts); rub-ons (Fancy Pants); decorative scissors (Fiskars); Misc: ink, tag

AHA!

Invest in a paper trimmer with decorative blades to make cutting decorative edges a piece of cake.

so thoughtful

[6]

Laying a straight title doesn't need to put you in a straight jacket.

3/08
During the winter, we have many movie nights. Everyone in their jammies, a big bowl of popcorn and a cozy blanket equals great family time!

family

MOVIE night

great fun

GOOD TIMES

Laying a straight title can be tricky (especially if you're a perfectionist!). Thinking about it gives me visions of trying to un-stick unruly letters. What's the simple solution? Using a straightedge and mat with a grid helps you lay a title that is tidy and straight. For a perfectly straight title, use a magnetic mat to keep the straightedge (and title) from slipping and make sure the mat is larger than your layout.

Supplies: Cardstock (WorldWin); patterned paper (BoBunny, Cosmo Cricket, Making Memories); title letters (American Crafts, We R Memory Keepers); chipboard accents (Making Memories); Misc: corner rounder, ink

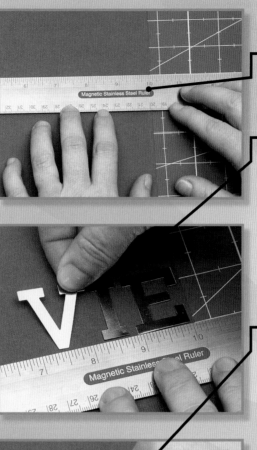

1. Set mat and ruler

Place your background on the magnetic mat, and set the top of the straightedge where you want your title to go.

2. Place letters

Place your letters with the bottom edges touching the top of the ruler. It's as simple as that!

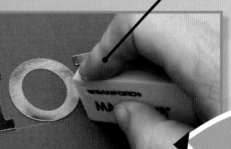

Try it another way

If you don't have a magnetic mat, you can still lay a straight title. Place your background on a regular grid-lined craft mat and draw a faint line in pencil along the straightedge. Place the bottoms of the letters along the pencil line. Once all the letters are placed, erase the pencil line using a white eraser.

Materials

metal straightedge
(longer than your layout)

magnetic craft mat with grid lines
(larger than your layout)

title letters

(optional) pencil and white eraser

AHA!

Pat the backs of letter stickers on your shirt or pants before assembling a title. This reduces their stickiness, so you don't have to commit to a title placement right away.

Secret

[7]

Using transparencies to hold a title or journaling is clearly a good idea.

Meet Grant the "Muffin Man". At the age of 10 he has become quite a wonderful helper in the kitchen. He often offers to help cook dinner especially when it's chili, his favorite. Lately he has turned his attention to baking. Sure he will make cookies but his specialty is muffins. Seems this summer we made lots because they were the perfect carbohydrate fuel for soccer games and now he wants to make them all the time. Currently there are several packages of blueberry muffin mix in the pantry just waiting for Grant "the muffin man" to get baking. October 2007

Envision this scenario: After realizing your oh-so-carefully placed title was in the wrong place, you unstick it, leaving a torn-up background in its wake. How do you avoid this situation? Easy. Attach your title to a transparency. It not only allows you to make sure the title is straight, but it also lets you move the title around the page before deciding where to place it. Add rub-ons and other details like Summer did here, and then staple the transparency to your layout. This technique also works well for journaling blocks when you don't want to print computer-generated words directly on the background.

Supplies: Cardstock (WorldWin); patterned paper, rub-ons (We R Memory Keepers); letter stickers, ribbon (American Crafts); word stickers (7gypsies); die-cuts (Doodlebug); felt (Fancy Pants); Misc: staples, transparency

Artwork by Summer Fullerton

1. Place letters on transparency

Lay a transparency on a craft mat with a grid. The mat will make it very easy to measure and lay out a straight title. You can also lay the transparency on any sheet of paper with parallel lines. Add your title letters to the transparency.

2. Add embellishments

Add embellishments to your title as desired. Rub-ons can be applied to slick surfaces like transparencies, so go ahead and add some designs. You can also add glitter, brads, felt shapes, stickers—whatever embellishments you want to dress up your title.

3. Attach title to layout

Cut out the title area of your transparency. Then determine where you want it on your layout and staple it on. Alternatively, you can attach the transparency with brads or eyelets.

Materials

transparency
craft mat with grid lines
title letters
rub-ons and embellishments
stapler

AHA!

For no-show adhesive under transparencies, use a specially designed adhesive tape runner for vellum like that from Therm O Web.

You can hand-cut any font you want without a die-cutting machine.

You can add the perfect font to your page's title with a little hand cutting. Here, I backed cut-out black cardstock with a piece of bright orange cardstock to give the title a jack-o-lantern glow. An intricate title with exactly the right font doesn't require a die-cutting machine. All you need are your favorite chipboard letters or computer and image-editing software.

Supplies: Cardstock (WorldWin); chipboard arrow (Fancy Pants); letters used as stencils (American Crafts); glossy topcoat (Ranger); Misc: ink

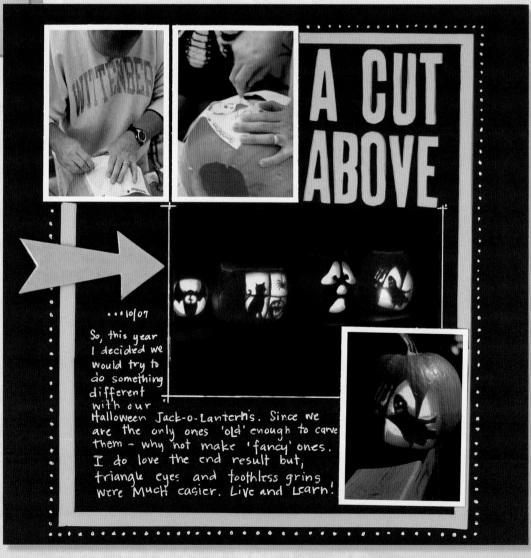

A CUT ABOVE

···10/07

So, this year I decided we would try to do something different with our Halloween Jack-o-Lanterns. Since we are the only ones 'old' enough to carve them - why not make 'fancy' ones. I do love the end result but, triangle eyes and toothless grins were much easier. Live and Learn!

USING CHIPBOARD LETTERS

1. Set chipboard letters on cardstock
If you're using the cardstock with the letters missing (like I did on my layout), place the chipboard letters where you'd like your title to be on your layout. If you're using the letters you cut, you can place the chipboard letters anywhere on the cardstock. Trace the chipboard letters.

2. Cut out letters
Place your cardstock on the craft mat, and cut out the letters along the pencil mark using a craft knife. If you are using the negative side, be careful to make clean cuts. Also be sure to save any "middle" parts, like the triangle inside an A or the circle inside an O.

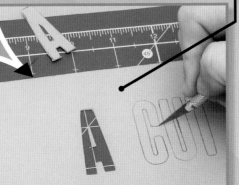

Materials
chipboard letters
pencil
cardstock
craft knife
craft mat

USING PHOTOSHOP ELEMENTS

1. Type and flip title
If you don't have any chipboard letters handy, or prefer a specific font, you can print a word backwards and cut it out. To flip a word using Photoshop Elements, create a new layer in Photoshop and type your word. Then go to Image>Rotate>Flip Horizontal to flip the word backwards.

2. Print and cut title
Print the backwards word on cardstock. Then cut out the letters as described in Step 2 above.

Materials
Adobe Photoshop Elements
printer
cardstock
craft knife
craft mat

[9]

Using rub-ons doesn't have to rub you the wrong way.

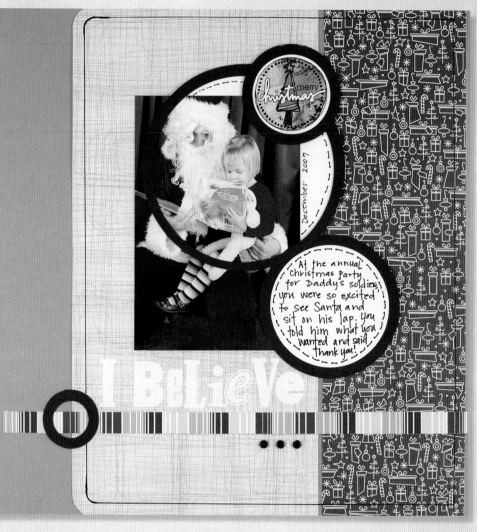

December 2007

merry christmas

At the annual christmas party for Daddy's soldiers you were so excited to see Santa and sit on his lap. You told him what you wanted and said thank you!

I BeLieVe

AHA!

Staple rub-on sheets to their backings to prevent rub-ons from going astray in storage.

We all know how to use a craft stick to add rub-ons to a layout. And we all know that applying rub-ons can be a pain. Some rub-ons are stubborn and refuse to stick to a page, while others are renegade and go on where you don't want them to. Adding a simple sentiment or design element doesn't have to make you cringe. With knowledge of a few tips and tricks, you'll be rubbing away all that frustration.

Supplies: Cardstock (WorldWin); patterned paper (KI Memories, Pebbles, Scenic Route); sticker (Memories Complete); rub-on (We R Memory Keepers); brads (Creative Impressions)

1. Cut out rub-on

Use micro-tip scissors to cut out the image that you want to use from its sheet. The scissors' small blades will make it easier to cut in between the tight spaces on the sheet. And don't try and skip this step! Rubbing an image attached to an entire sheet makes for good odds of getting unintended rub-ons all over your project.

2. Remove backing

Don't forget to remove the backing! This step may seem obvious, but if you're in a rush, this step is easy to overlook. So, if your rub-on is not actually rubbing on, don't curse it. Instead, make sure to check that your backing has been removed.

3. Rub on image

Start in one section of the image and rub with a stylus or craft stick until that section is rubbed on entirely. You can lift up the rub-on sheet to check. As you rub, be sure to hold down the entire image with your other hand so that it doesn't slide while you're rubbing one part. I like to use a wooden craft stick or sturdy plastic stylus to rub because they don't bend while I'm fiercely rubbing.

4. Remove rub-on if needed

Don't like the rub-on? Put it in the wrong place? No worries! Lay a piece of transparent tape over the image. Gently rub the tape onto the image and slowly lift it to remove the rub-on. Repeat until the unwanted image is completely removed.

Materials

micro-tip scissors
rub-on sheet
wooden craft stick or stylus
background paper
(optional) transparent tape

Secret [10]

There's not only one right way to mix patterns—but there is an easy way.

Working with patterned paper can be both fun and challenging. Finding an effective way to balance and mix the different patterns is the key to building a great page. There's not one correct way to mix patterns; often it's just personal preference. But some methods for combining patterns are quicker to master than others. Lisa follows one simple formula that you can use for creating a successful layout.

Supplies: Cardstock (WorldWin); patterned paper (Scenic Route); chipboard letters (BasicGrey); journaling blocks (Maya Road); felt (Creative Imaginations); Misc: brads

the way you cartwheel and tumble all over the house.

that you are insanely ticklish!

your incredible sense of humor.

I LOVE...

Artwork by Lisa Dorsey

1. Choose multi-colored pattern

Start by choosing a pattern with several different colors, like this circle print in orange, green and white. Then pick two colors from the pattern; choose one to act as the main color and one to act as the accent color. On this layout, orange is the main color while green is the accent color.

2. Choose main color pattern

Choose one or two patterns in your main color. You will apply these patterns in the largest proportion on the layout. The patterns should be tone-on-tone prints like these orange polka dot and flower patterns.

3. Choose accent color pattern

Choose a pattern that contains your accent color. Since you will apply this pattern in a relatively small proportion, you can chose a multi-colored pattern like this blue and green print, or use a tone-on-tone pattern.

Materials
3-4 patterned papers

AHA!

After finishing a layout, use the paper scraps left on your workspace to make a generic card. That way, you'll always have an extra card during the inevitable moments of last-minute need!

Supplies: Patterned paper (BasicGrey); stamps (Cornish Heritage Farms); brads (Making Memories); Misc: ink, thread

Artwork by Kim Hughes

You can alter any kind of chipboard to match your patterned paper.

Artwork by Sherry Steveson

I never realized how few photos I have of Madison with her Dad. I am so glad I have these precious moments of closeness of these two. 09/2006

A priceless photo

AHA!

When sanding chipboard, sand from top to bottom to avoid tearing edges or lifting up layers.

You have a pile of raw or mismatched chipboard pieces waiting to be used. What are you to do with them? Cover them with patterend paper to complement any layout! Here, Sherry covered a chipboard flourish with patterned paper to liven up her simple page. You can also use patterned paper that coordinates with other prints on your layout.

Supplies: Cardstock (WorldWin); patterned paper (Paper Trunk); chipboard shapes (Rusty Pickle); rub-ons (Daisy D's, Urban Lily)

1. Apply adhesive to chipboard

If you are using a finished chipboard piece, sand the chipboard so the adhesive will stick easily. Then apply adhesive to the front of the chipboard. Brush liquid adhesive like decoupage medium on the piece so that all the edges will stick to the patterned paper. You can also use a glue stick, as this will also apply adhesive along the edges.

2. Cut paper away from chipboard

Place the wet chipboard piece face down onto the back of a sheet of patterned paper. Let the adhesive dry completely before starting to cut. (If the adhesive is still wet, the piece is likely to slip around as you cut.) Using the craft knife, cut off the excess paper around the chipboard piece.

3. Sand outer edges of chipboard

Sanding the edges of your chipboard will not only give it a textured, distressed look, but will soften the edges and hide any uneven cuts. You can use a sanding sponge to sand the edges, but a piece of fine-grit sandpaper does the job just as well.

4. Sand inner edges of chipboard

A sanding sponge or sanding files will have a hard time getting into tight spaces. If you're having trouble, use a thin sanding tool (like this one from BasicGrey) to sand inside the nooks and crannies.

Materials

chipboard piece
sanding sponge or sandpaper
paintbrush
decoupage medium or glue stick
patterned paper
craft knife
craft mat
thin sanding tool

Choosing the right stamping ink doesn't have to be a mystery.

Stamping is a fun technique to use on your projects, but determining the right ink to use on a surface can be difficult without a little guidance. Knowing the types of inks and their uses will help you follow Kim's example and stamp on everything from patterned paper and cardstock to photos and transparencies.

Supplies: Cardstock (WorldWin); patterned paper (Dream Street, Fancy Pants); stamps (Cornish Heritage Farms); flowers (Making Memories, Prima); button (Autumn Leaves); transparency (Hambly); Misc: embossing powder, inks, sandpaper

the world of discovery

we had a blast on your field trip while you learned about your 5 senses

Artwork by Kim Hughes

CHALK INK: USE ON PAPER FOR A SOFT LOOK

Ink edges

Chalk ink is great for inking edges of papers because it dries with a soft look. Simply run the ink pad along the edge of the paper. Angle the pad toward the page for more ink on the page and away for less. Keep in mind that chalk inks dry quickly on paper but don't dry on slick surfaces.

Stamp image

Chalk ink works well for images that you want to have a soft look. It's great for embellishing baby-themed layouts or for pages with a vintage style.

Materials

chalk ink
stamp

AHA!

After stamping, clean a stamp quickly by wiping it with a baby wipe. Keep a tub at your desk!

little sweetie

Inking edges with chalk ink not only gives cards an overall soft look, but gives edges definition when papers are layered. Here, black ink helps the pastel papers pop.

Supplies: Cardstock (WorldWin); patterned paper (Autumn Leaves); brad, letter stickers (Making Memories); chipboard (Scenic Route); scoring tool (EK Success)

Artwork by Kim Hughes

PIGMENT INK: USE ON THICK PAPER

Stamp on cardstock
Pigment ink stamps a clean image on paper. It's much thicker than other inks and stays wet longer, so using a thick paper (like cardstock) works best with this ink. Pigment ink can be heat-set to help the ink dry and to prevent the image from smearing.

PIGMENT INK: USE FOR HEAT EMBOSSING

1. Stamp image and apply embossing powder
Because it is thick and slow to dry, pigment ink is the best option for heat embossing. Stamp your image, then immediately pour embossing powder onto the stamped image. Dump off all the extra powder onto another sheet of paper. Gently tap the paper with your fingers to remove all stray embossing powder.

2. Apply heat gun to melt powder
Hold the heat gun close to the embossed image. Be careful not to hold the heat in one place for too long. The heat will melt the embossing powder and leave a raised, glossy image.

Heat embossing can give a dramatic effect. Here Kim uses white embossing against a black background. This embossed, raised image just begs to be touched.

Supplies: Patterned paper (My Mind's Eye); stamps (BasicGrey, Cornish Heritage Farms); brads (Imaginisce); ribbon (Beaux Regards); Misc: embossing powder

Artwork by Kim Hughes

with
Sympathy

AHA!

For easy, precise inking of edges, use a small ink pad like the chalk ink pads from ColorBox.

Materials

solvent ink
stamp

SOLVENT INK: USE ON SLICK SURFACES OR UNDER WET MEDIA

Stamp on any surface

Solvent ink can be used on almost every surface. It leaves a crisp stamped image. Solvent inks are perfect for stamping on slick surfaces such as photos, transparencies and acrylic. Solvent inks also work well for stamped images over which you'll apply wet media like decoupage medium or paint. The solvent ink will not bleed or smear when the wet medium is brushed over the stamped image.

[13]

There is a right way to stamp images on photos.

Stamping on a photo adds a quick border, a little detail or a sweet sentiment. Here, Summer uses a flourish stamp to give her photos a fancy touch. As you know, stamping on photos takes a special ink. It also requires a soft touch with the stamp. When done right, stamping on photos adds a wonderful, unique look that can't be accomplished with dimensional embellishments.

Supplies: Cardstock (WorldWin); patterned paper (BasicGrey, Fontwerks); tag (Making Memories); felt (Fancy Pants); brad (Imaginisce); stamp (Inque Boutique); decorative scissors (Fiskars); cutting system (Xyron); Misc: ink

our Mermaid

Today we arrived at Fort Stevens the sun was shining so we headed down to explore the beach for a bit. Brad and Corinne sat down and buried each other's feet in the sand. Then they decided to make Corinne into a mermaid by forming her buried feet into the shape of a fin. Even Grant got into the act. They packed sand and formed her tail for about half an hour until it was just right. They added the scale detail and Corinne the mermaid was complete.

7/07 Fort Stevens, OR

Favorite Activities to do...
ON THE BEACH...

Artwork by Summer Fullerton

1. Stamp image

Acrylic stamps are best for stamping on photos—they make it easy to see exactly where your stamped image is going to be so you don't cover up an important part of your photo. To stamp, ink the stamp as you normally would (using the solvent ink). Then place the stamp down on the photo and hold it down for a second or two; do not rock the stamp—it could slip and blur your image.

2. Lift up stamp

Hold your photo in place while lifting the stamp off. The photo may stick to the stamp or slide as you are trying to lift the stamp, causing a blurred image.

Remove a stamped image

You can remove solvent ink from slick surfaces with adhesive remover (such as Un-Du) and a paper towel. The adhesive remover will not ruin your photo. It may look as if it is discoloring the photo, but, as it dries, the color of the photo will return.

Materials

photo
solvent ink
acrylic stamp with block
(optional) adhesive remover (Un-Du)
paper towel

AHA!

Store ink pads upside down to keep the ink at the surface of the pad for the best stamping.

Did you ever think to use photos to decorate cards? Add a family photo to a holiday card or a simple picture to send a note. With solvent ink, you can stamp your sentiment directly on the photo for a one-of-a-kind creation.

Supplies: Cardstock (WorldWin); patterned paper (BasicGrey, Webster's Pages); decorative cardstock (KI Memories); buttons (Autumn Leaves); acrylic snowflakes (Heidi Swapp); ribbon (Beaux Regards); stamp (Cornish Heritage Farms); Misc: ink

Artwork by Kim Hughes

[14]

Piercing holes will give you a hand in stitching.

a boy lives here

5/07
Andrew was told to put his new baseball some place safe. I found it in my bowl of potpourri. That's not exactly what I meant but, no one bothered it there.

Stitching adds detail dimension to a layout, and hand-stitching allows flexibility and freedom that sewing with a machine can't. But with hand-sewing can come uneven stitches, crooked lines and odd shapes. Guess what? You can stitch a perfect circle like my red circle here—without frustration! The secret to hand-stitching is pre-poked holes so you know exactly where to place your stitches.

Supplies: Cardstock (WorldWin); patterned paper (KI Memories); letter stickers (American Crafts); Misc: floss

AHA!

For easy piercing, place a piece of craft foam or an old mouse pad under a project.

1. Trace shape

Trace the design you want to stitch using the pencil. I like to use chipboard leftovers as a stencil. If you'd like to free-hand draw your design, go for it!

2. Poke holes

Poke holes along the pencil line with a paper piercer or a thumbtack. Holes should be about 1/8" (3mm) apart. Then erase your pencil lines.

3. Stitch shape

To stitch, first thread your needle with three strands of floss. Then use the holes as a guide for backstitching. To backstitch, pull your needle up through the first hole from the back of the paper to the front, then push your needle down through the second hole. Then pull the needle up through the third hole, and then back down through the second hole.

Materials

paper
pencil
stencil (like a chipboard negative)
thumbtack or paper piercer
floss (three strands)
needle

A card is personal by nature, so hand stitching, with its personal touch, is a perfect addition to a homemade card. On this card, Melissa simply stitched a border around a paper embellishment, showing that even the simplest stitches add a unique quality.

Supplies: Cardstock (WorldWin); chipboard, patterned paper, sticker, trim (Melissa Frances); tag (7gypsies); buttons (Making Memories); Misc: floss, ink

Artwork by Melissa Phillips

You can prevent madness when attaching tiny eyelets and brads.

Supplies: Cardstock (WorldWin); flowers, patterned paper, ribbon (Making Memories); stickers (Scenic Route); transparency (Hambly); brads (American Crafts)

Thanksgiving 2007

JUST 1

All I wanted was just 1 decent photo of the two of you together on thanksgiving Day. Andrew was ready but, Laura really had no interest in participating. After a dozen or so shots, Laura finally loosend up and started to smile. Thankfully I did get 1 good one!

Many times the mere thought of going to the trouble to add brads or eyelets to your layout will make you tremble. But sometimes using eyelets and brads is the best solution, like on this layout. Transparencies add a beautiful touch, but without brads or eyelets, attaching them them to your page without visible adhesive can be tricky. The good news is that using the best practices for adding eyelets and brads will set you at ease.

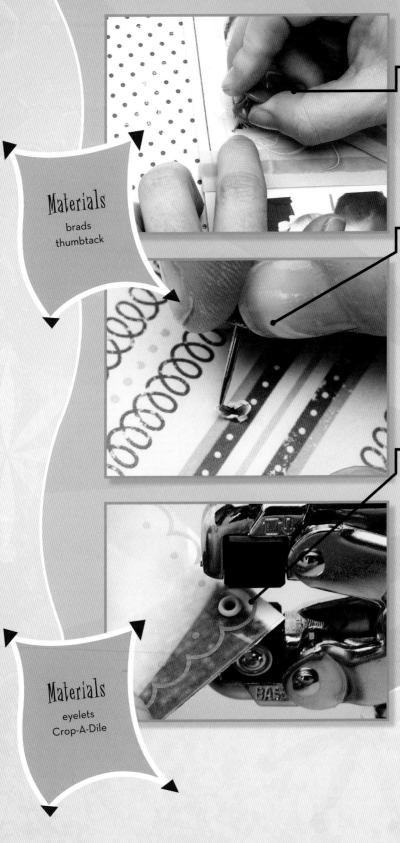

ATTACHING BRADS

Substitute with a thumbtack

If you don't have a paper piercer, grab a thumbtack off your bulletin board and use it to punch holes for tiny brads. Thumbtacks are also useful in place of anywhere punches when you need a hole in the middle of a page.

Materials
brads
thumbtack

Open brad prongs with a thumbtack

Those tight, tiny prongs on brads can be so frustrating to open! Use the thumbtack instead of your fingers to squeeze in between and open up the prongs.

INSERTING EYELETS

Use a Crop-A-Dile

Getting out the hole punch, craft mat and hammer is a hassle. To easily apply any size eyelet, use a Crop-A-Dile. Just punch once to make a hole and punch again to attach the eyelet. Need to know the right way to use a Crop-A-Dile? It's simple. There are two moveable cubes on the Crop-A-Dile. The cube with the "pointy" ends always goes on top when setting an eyelet. Set the eyelet so the pointy end goes through the hole in the top of the eyelet, and you're good to go.

Materials
eyelets
Crop-A-Dile

AHA!

Stitching is also an attractive way to attach transparencies. When sewing multiple layers with a machine, use a heavyweight needle meant for denim.

white

Sands

.may 2007.

You will hit the sand and run as soon as we got there. I was really surprised at how daring you were mad! New Mexico

Easier Ways
SECRETS TO SIMPLER SCRAPPING

chapter 2

Whether you're focused on trying new techniques or just getting photos in albums, you're bound to want to find a hassle-free way to scrap faster. With as many ways as there are to get things done, there is always an easier way to complete even simple tasks (like arranging photos). In this chapter, I'll tell you all about the shortcuts I've put into practice on most of my projects.

Secret

[16]

Using a punch
is the easiest
way to crop
photos to the
same size.

Want even more photos on your pages? Do what Summer did and print out wallet-sized photos, and then use a punch to crop the photos to the same size. On this layout, Summer used the small square photos along with patterned paper punched from the same square punch for a graphic look. The arrangement provides a great way to share a photo essay of all of the Christmas decorations she displays throughout her house.

Supplies: Cardstock (WorldWin); patterned paper (BasicGrey, Scenic Route); letter and word stickers (American Crafts, Heidi Swapp); die-cut shapes, stickers (Scenic Route); brad, tag (Making Memories); Misc: paint, square punch

Artwork by Summer Fullerton

Punch photos

Insert your photo face down into the punch. Turn the punch over so you can see exactly what area of your photo you are punching. Now, just squeeze!

Materials

photo
square punch (1½"–2" [4cm x 5cm])

smile

AHA!

Punches are always great to have on hand, whether for cropping photos or for adding simple details, like this yellow circle, to projects. But it's annoying when punches start to stick. If that happens, punch through wax paper to lubricate the cutting blade.

Supplies: Cardstock (WorldWin); patterned paper (BoBunny, Fontwerks); sticker (Sandylion); stamps (Autumn Leaves, Inkadinkado); chipboard (Making Memories); brads (American Crafts); paper punch (EK Success); Misc: ink

Secret

[17]

Going black and white will keep the focus on the photos.

The great thing about holidays is all the different photos we usually have of them. The bad thing is that sometimes very colorful photos compete with busy background papers, or they simply don't match in hue. You don't have to struggle to make it work; just make your photos black-and-white using image-editing or word-processing software. Set against the colors in the Halloween paper, these black-and-white photos on Paula's layout take center stage, allowing her kids' trick-or-treating, and not the crazy colors, to be the focus.

Supplies: Cardstock (WorldWin); die-cut shapes, patterned paper, rub-on (Daisy D's)

Artwork by Paula Gilarde

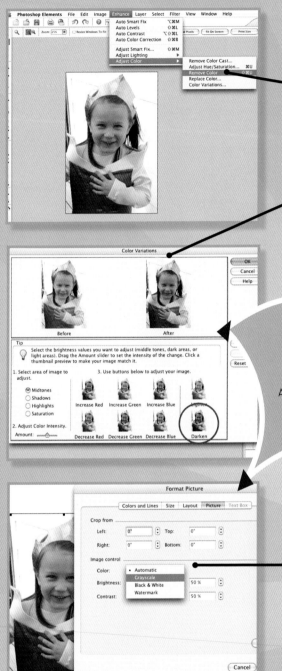

USING PHOTOSHOP ELEMENTS TO REMOVE COLOR

1. Open file and remove color
Open your digital photo in Photoshop Elements. Then go to Enhance>Adjust Color>Remove Color. If you're satisfied with the look of the photo, stop here. If not, go to Step 2 for a one-step click to sharpen the photo a bit.

2. Adjust darkness
Go to Enhance>Adjust Color>Color Variations. When the box opens, click on the photo at the bottom right of the screen labeled Darken. A preview of your new, darkened photo will show up at the top of the screen. Click OK.

Materials
digital photo
Adobe Photoshop Elements

USING MICROSOFT WORD TO GO BLACK AND WHITE

Insert photo and format
Insert your photo into a blank Word document (Insert>Picture>From File). Then go to Format>Picture. After the box opens, click on the Picture tab if it's not already selected. Under Image Color, click on the Color drop-down menu and choose Grayscale. (Do not choose Black & White.) You can also adjust the brightness and contrast if desired.

Materials
digital photo
Microsoft Word

AHA!
You don't have to force yourself to use themed paper for holiday layouts if they just won't work for a page.

51

[18]

With flexible rulers, you can "wave" good-bye to free-hand curves.

Waves and curves add movement to a page. The curves on this layout are what draw your eye down to Summer's journaling. A flexible ruler (like Bo Bunny's) is an easy way to trace a wave onto cardstock. Wait a minute: Isn't drawing a curve freehand just as easy as tracing a ruler? Not exactly. The secret here is that bending a ruler to create a wave lets you plan ahead. Shape and reshape your wave on the ruler until you get it right—and before you even set pencil to paper. The ruler also helps you trace the same wave over and over again.

Supplies: Cardstock (WorldWin); patterned paper (Making Memories); chipboard letters, tab (Heidi Swapp); die-cuts (Doodlebug); rub-on (We R Memory Keepers)

the WALK

We drove by the pool several days in a row and didn't even know it was there. It was hiding ever so perfectly behind a dark fence and several huge trees. But when the temperatures rose we were sure glad we found it.

I don't think we intended to spend more than an hour swimming that day, but one hour turned into several. And I had to drag you away from the water kicking and screaming.

After a long day frolicking in the sun swimming and splashing at the pool I don't blame you for dreading the long wet walk back to the house.

Corinne August 2005
Hartstene Island, WA

Artwork by Summer Fullerton

1. Shape ruler
Bend the ruler until you achieve the shape you want. Set it down on the background to check the placement. Reshape as needed.

2. Trace wave and cut out
Lightly trace along the edge of the ruler with the pencil. Be sure to hold down the ruler with your hand so it doesn't move or change shape as you trace. Cut out the wave, and then erase any remaining pencil marks.

Materials
flexible ruler
cardstock
pencil
scissors
white eraser

AHA!
Make layouts look neat and tidy by cleaning up stray adhesive. You can make the task easy with a special adhesive remover tool such as the one from EK Success.

You know that a flexible ruler helps create one large wave along the edge of a page. But with its flexibility, you can also use it to trace multiple, smaller waves like the edge of the watermelon on Kim's layout. With a flexible ruler, the flexible possibilities are endless!

Supplies: Cardstock (WorldWin); patterned paper (Dream Street); brads (American Crafts); paper punch (Martha Stewart); paper trim (Doodlebug); cutting system (Xyron)

Artwork by Kim Moreno

A slice of cold watermelon on a hot summer day, is there anything better than that?

enjoy

Summer

Secret

[19]

A pen and straightedge make a quick and simple border.

Drawing a line somewhere on my layouts has fast become one of my favorite ways to frame a photo or entire page. Even the simplest of lines helps ground various layout elements and pulls everything together. Here the double-line frame was a quick way to draw the eye in and frame the photos, title and journaling. Plus, the simple sketched look of the frame coordinates well with my school-themed page.

1st DAY

Pre-K

1st day of Pre-K! So excited to see friends from last year and anxious to learn so many new things! Ready for a great year!

Andrew

Andrew 4½

Sept. 2007

Supplies: Patterned paper (Creative Imaginations); letters (American Crafts, Reminisce); sticker (Autumn Leaves); tab (Melissa Frances); paper punch (Stampin' Up)

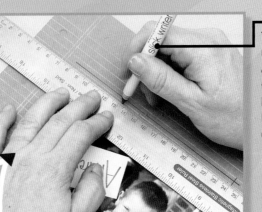

Trace straightedge

Using the straightedge as a guide, draw a line to create a border on the page. You can draw a second line to create a double border. For a casual look, cross the lines unevenly at the four corners.

Materials

pen
straightedge

You can leave a border unadorned like I did on my layout (on the previous page), and it will still highlight the focus of your layout. Add brads to the corners of a thick-lined frame as Janelle did here, and dress up your page.

Supplies: Patterned paper (American Crafts, Around the Block, Making Memories); letter stickers (SEI); stickers (7gypsies, Jenni Bowlin, KI Memories, Making Memories); brads (Doodlebug)

AHA!

An easy way to get parallel lines without a large craft mat is to use a T-square. Just line up the top of the T with one side of your layout.

Artwork by Janelle Richmond

[20]

Creating faux stitching is "sew" easy.

It's winter time and cocoa time!
Except - Andrew only wants *warm* cocoa.
Oh, and NO marshmellows. Despite these little reminders everytime I make cocoa... This kid lights up like a christmas tree when anyone mentions cocoa!

keep warm

winter

{mmm}
*hot cocoa

'/06

AHA!

No need to always measure with a ruler. Create a gorgeous layout and no one will ever know if you eyeballed a measurement!

Hand-stitching adds charm and detail to a layout, but with the needle threading and all that floss you need to make it around a large layout, it's not the quickest technique to accomplish. Even if you know the best way to hand-stitch (see page 43!), there's an easier way: faux stitching. Faux stitching is simply faking the look of stitches using a thumbtack and pen. As you can see on this layout, it's a quick and easy solution for a homespun border with a lasting impact.

Supplies: Patterned paper (KI Memories, Sassafras Lass); letter stickers (American Crafts, EK Success); stickers (KI Memories)

1. Draw line or shape

With a straightedge and pencil, lightly draw a line (or shape) on your paper where you want the stitching to be. Here, I'm drawing a border.

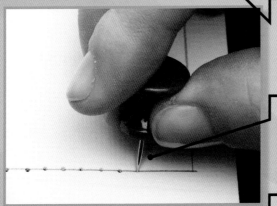

2. Pierce holes

Use the tip of a thumbtack to pierce holes along the pencil line about every ¼" (6mm). (A thumbtack or needle will make the tiniest holes.)

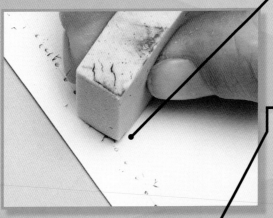

3. Erase pencil marks

Erase your pencil lines with a white eraser, which is best for removing marks without damaging the paper. Make sure the pencil marks are erased thoroughly, as half the spaces between the holes will not be concealed.

4. Draw stitches

To create a faux running stitch (shown on my layout), draw a line in pen to connect the first two holes. Then draw a line to connect the next pair of holes. There should be a space between your stitches. To create a faux backstitch—even easier!—simply draw a line connecting all the holes.

[21]

Using a circle cutter gives you precision-cut rings.

Circles seemed like the perfect embellishment to go along with the goofy faces Papa was making as Andrew took his picture. In fact, circles—and rings made from cutting circles—make great additions to a variety of layout themes. But what do you do to create precisely round circles that are bigger than your punch? Don't go freehand or cut a traced shape. Use a circle cutter—the right way. It's the way to make it easier.

Supplies: Cardstock (WorldWin); chipboard shapes, patterned paper, sticker (American Crafts); letter stickers (Arctic Frog); circle cutter (Creative Memories)

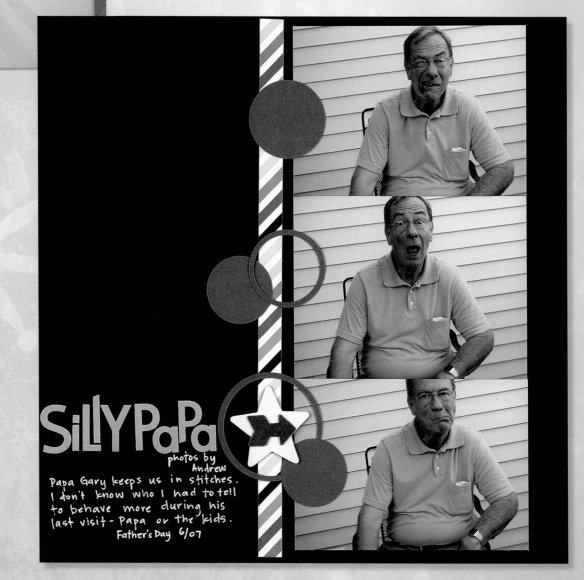

SillyPaPa
photos by Andrew

Papa Gary keeps us in stitches. I don't know who I had to tell to behave more during his last visit - Papa or the kids.
Father's Day 6/07

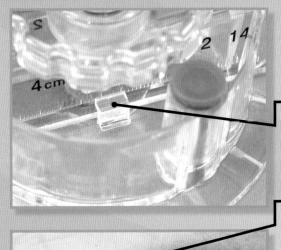

1. Set circle diameter

To set the diameter (length across) of the circle, slide the arm of the cutter (in and out) so that the number lines up with the transparent arrow on the cutter. Don't remove the orange cap at the bottom of the cutter.

2. Cut first circle

Press down firmly with your hand to hold the cutter in place. Some people get the best rotation and grip if they stand up, so you can give that a try. Rotate the arm of the cutter with your other hand until you cut a complete circle. Stop applying pressure on the handle, but keep the center in place. If you want just a circle, stop here. To create a ring, continue to Step 3.

3. Cut inside circle

Increase the diameter of the circle slightly without lifting the cutter (this keeps the center of the cutter in place). Repeat Step 2 until you complete the circle. Pop out the center to use both the ring and the center circle on your layout.

Materials

circle cutter (Fiskars)
paper
cutting mat

AHA!

Make hand-cutting a little easier by using a glass mat. A glass mat has a smooth surface to allow the cutting blade to slide easily across. Don't have a glass mat? Simply use a piece of glass from an old picture frame.

[22]

There's a backwards way to make your title fit.

Coming up with titles is only half the battle. The other half is making sure you have enough room for the title on your layout. Of course, if you start from the left edge, you know your title won't run off the edge of the page. But fitting a title on the right side of a layout is easy too with Katrina's simple trick: Place the letters in reverse order from the right edge. Splitting a title into multiple lines, as Katrina did, also helps ensure a proper fit.

Supplies: Cardstock (WorldWin); patterned paper (We R Memory Keepers); rub-ons (American Crafts, BasicGrey); die-cut (Daisy D's); brads (BoBunny, Making Memories); Misc: ink

home is where the heart is

I never want to forget…
the cowboys hats that you wear.
the way that you laugh
when you (still) tickle me.
the sound of your pickup
coming up the road.
the afternoon coffee breaks at the
Dairy Queen with your buddies.
But most of all…
I never want to forget how much
I love you

GRANDPA BOB

Artwork by Katrina Simeck

Start with last letter

To make sure a title will fit on your page, start on the farthest edge and work right to left. Place the last letter of the title near the edge and work backward from there. Here, I'm using rub-on letters, but this technique works with any kind of letter.

Materials

letters

AHA!

Sometimes a rub-on doesn't always rub on—it's pretty easy to end up with a broken design. Instead of starting over you can use a pen in a color that matches your rub-on and fill in the missing part.

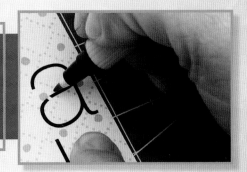

You can place your title backward from the edge of an element—like a photo or journaling block—as well. The principle is the same, plus is makes for a more interesting design. If you forget to start backward and run out of room, follow Kim's lead and place letters over your photo. People will think you designed it that way on purpose!

Supplies: Patterned paper (Dream Street); buttons (Autumn Leaves); brads (Creative Impressions); cutting system (Xyron)

Artwork by Kim Moreno

[23]

The right tools
make it a snap
to insert brads
in chipboard.

white
Sands

·may 2007·

*You all in the sand run-
ning as soon as we got
there. I was really surp-
rised at how daring you
were Madi! New Mexico*

Artwork by Kim Moreno

AHA!

Stuck on what background color to
choose? Go with white—it provides a
clean surface that matches any layout
theme and makes photos pop.

Brads are always a great addition to a layout, whether they're
adding visual interest or attaching an element to a page. Here, Kim
uses brads to embellish a chipboard tab. Wait, adding brads to
chipboard—isn't that more trouble than it's worth? It's not the brad
that's the trouble, but the hole. Technically, a standard hole punch
will punch through chipboard, but it's such a hassle; you have to
have the might of an entire army to get that hole punched ... and if
the blade is dull, forget it! Well, there's an easier way—even more
than one! With the right tools you can do the impossible.

Supplies: Cardstock (WorldWin); patterned paper (Sassafras Lass); brads, letter stickers
(American Crafts); rub-ons (Hambly, American Crafts); chipboard (Magistical Memories);
decorative trimmer (Creative Memories)

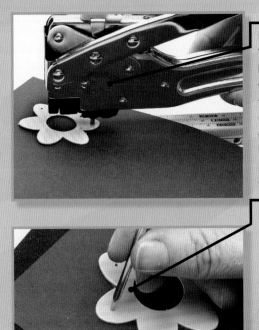

Use a Crop-A-Dile

Without a doubt the easiest way to make a hole in chipboard is with a Crop-A-Dile (or the Crop-A-Dile II Big Bite, like I used here). With this monster tool, just punch to get a hole in no time. Here's another secret: Adhere the chipboard to the background before punching holes so that both the chipboard and the background get punched at once without the chipboard slipping.

Use a paper piercer

It may seem contrary, but even though it makes a smaller hole, using a paper piercer is actually easier than using a hole punch. The piercer's sharp tip slides right through the chipboard. To make a hole big enough for a brad, poke one hole and then anther right next to it. After poking the second hole, wiggle the piercer around to widen the hole.

Materials
chipboard
Crop-A-Dile or
paper piercer

Eyelets add the same detail and work the same as brads in attaching elements to layouts. They also dress up chipboard as well as brads do, as you can see on this sweet card. Luckily, the Crop-A-Dile sets eyelets in a snap. (See page 45 for the how-to.)

Supplies: Cardstock (WorldWin); patterned paper (Scenic Route); die-cut (Doodlebug); chipboard accent (Making Memories); eyelets, punch (We R Memory Keepers); ribbon (Rusty Pickle)

Secret

[24]

A set of brads
can line up
easily.

Now you know that there's an easier way to add brads to thick chipboard. But is there a way to line up multiple brads? Yes! On background paper or embellishments, you can ensure your brads are evenly spaced—and easily. Now you can create a layout like mine with rows of brads that provide an interesting look. The orange accents are perfect for this story about picking citrus fruit.

Supplies: Cardstock (WorldWin); patterned paper (Creative Imaginations, My Mind's Eye); chipboard letters (Pressed Petals); letter stickers (American Crafts); chipboard accent (Making Memories); brads (Creative Impressions); stickers (Creative Imaginations); dimensional adhesive (JudiKins); Misc: ink

  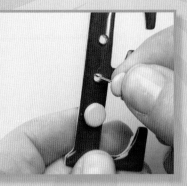

1. Arrange brads upside down

Lay brads upside down on your paper or embellishment to make sure your spacing will be correct once they are inserted into holes. Off to the side of the brads, mark where the center of each one will be. If you're workng with paper, mark the holes with a pencil. Use a thumbtack or paper piercer to mark tiny holes on surfaces that won't accept pencil, such as these epoxy-coated letters.

2. Mark and punch holes

Remove the brads and use the marks as a guide to mark holes where the brads should be inserted. Punch holes over the marks.

3. Insert brads in holes

Insert the brads. Then get excited that they are all lined up nice and neat and in the right place!

Materials

paper or embellishment
brads
thumbtack
paper piercer or pencil
Crop-A-Dile or hole punch

You can make setting a straight line of eyelets easy too! The steps are similar, starting with where each eyelet will go.

Supplies: Cardstock (WorldWin); chipboard shapes, patterned paper, rub-on (Crate Paper); decorative scissors (Fiskars); Misc: ink, eyelets

Thank you

AHA!

An inexpensive make-up sponge makes a great applicator for applying chalk ink along paper edges (like those on the card at left). Simply run the sponge on the ink pad and then draw it across the edges of your page.

Secret

[25]

Line up to get straight journaling.

Using your own handwriting can be unappealing for many reasons, not the least of which is trying to get the lines straight. An easy way to ensure your journaling doesn't run uphill or slide down your page is to draw lines on which you write your story. You don't even need to bother using a pencil and erasing the lines. Just do what Kim did and draw them in pen. Her visible, hand-drawn ink lines add a personal touch that complements the handwritten words.

the best

Anywhere we were or anytime there was music I could count on you to get up and dance with me! You're the best!

Amjie & Kim 4/05

dance partner ever!

Artwork by Kim Moreno

Supplies: Cardstock (WorldWin); patterned paper (Dream Street); letter stickers, rub-on letters (American Crafts); brads (American Crafts, Creative Impressions); die-cut (Doodlebug)

1. Draw lines
Set the page background on a craft mat with gridlines. Line up the straightedge across the page background; using a straightedge that is longer than your page will ensure journaling lines that are parallel with the page. Square up the paper and the straightedge with the gridlines on the mat and draw lines with a pen.

2. Write journaling
Write your story! If you really hate the idea of visible lines, simply follow the above steps, but write your lines in pencil and then erase the lines after you've finished journaling. Be sure to let the ink dry before erasing.

Try it another way
Want straight lines made even easier? Use a stamp with lines built right in.

Materials
paper
straightedge
craft mat with grid lines
pen

AHA!
To get a crisp stamped image from an acrylic stamp, place a mousepad under your paper before stamping.

Secret

[26]

Printing wallet-sized photos will help you get more pictures on a page.

Artwork by Summer Fullerton

AHA!

If your scissors start to stick due to cutting through adhesive, wipe them down with a cotton ball wet with adhesive remover (such as Un-Du).

We all have tons of photos from events, and it's usually hard to decide which ones will be used on a layout. The good news is you can use them all! And there's an easier way than doing all that cropping and cutting. Just use wallet-sized photos and see how simple it is to get multiple photos on one layout like Summer's. You can order wallet-sized photos from a professional photo developer or simply print your own photo strip like Summer did here. All you need is image-editing software and a printer.

Supplies: Cardstock (WorldWin); patterned paper (Making Memories, My Mind's Eye); chipboard and rub-on letters (Heidi Swapp); stickers (Daisy D's, My Mind's Eye); rhinestones (Doodlebug); Misc: paint

1. Resize and place photos

Open up all your photos in Photoshop and resize each to about 2" x 3" (5cm x 8cm). Then open a blank file that is 8½" (22cm) wide and 11" (28cm) high. One by one, drag the images into the blank file; click on the move tool (the arrow at the top of the toolbar on the left side of the screen), click your mouse on the photos and drag. Place the images right next to each other if you don't want a white border around them.

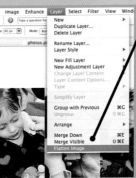

2. Flatten layers and print

When all the photos are placed, flatten the layers. Go to Layer>Flatten Image. Save your file and print it onto 8½" x 11" (22cm x 28cm) photo paper. Cut out the strip of photos.

Materials

Adobe Photoshop Elements
digital photos
printer
photo paper or cardstock

Using wallet-sized photos doesn't mean you have to use only wallet-sized photos. After taking many photos from my grandfather's funeral, I wanted to remember him and the beautiful flowers that were so carefully chosen for him by his family. With this many photos, the best option for me was to use a lot of wallet-sized prints with one larger, standard-sized photo to anchor them. Doing this keeps the main focus of the layout on the big photo but allows the reader to see multiple related photos.

Supplies: Patterned paper (BasicGrey, Making Memories); vellum (WorldWin); chipboard letters (American Crafts); brads (Doodlebug); die-cutting machine (Provo Craft)

Why waste time mounting your photos on cardstock? A great timesaver is printing your photos with a white edge border. Yvonne saved even more time by printing off multiple photos on one sheet and cutting them down with a bit of white left around each photo. This technique is made simple with the help of Photoshop Elements. If you line the photos up evenly using Photoshop, once printed, one slice of the paper trimmer will create perfectly even edges.

Supplies: Cardstock (WorldWin); stamps (Fiskars, Time Flies Design); Misc: ink

The Stages of Dance

The boys love to dance. It's always a joy to watch them tear up the carpet! This particular day I was able to stop the motion during Charlie's dance. The wonders of photography allowed me to truly see the joy in his face in each frame. He's a crazy little dancer.

{ March 2008 }

① dance
② be happy
③ laugh
④ be silly
⑤ smile
⑥ jump!

Artwork by Yvonne Busdeker

AHA!

If you don't have a photo printer at home, you can still print multiple pictures on one sheet. Just have your photo developer print the grouping as one 8" x 10" (20cm x 25cm) photo.

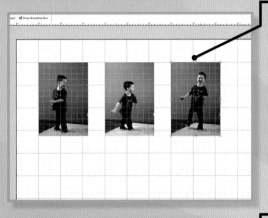

1. Open new file with grid

Open all your photos in Photoshop and resize them as needed. Then open a blank file that is 8½" (22cm) wide and 11" (28cm) high. Then go to View>Grid to make a grid appear on your page (the Grid option should have a check mark).

2. Arrange photos

One by one, drag the images into the blank file with the grid lines. To do this, click on the move tool (the arrow at the top of the toolbar), click your mouse on the photos and drag them. Place the first image so that it lines up with grid lines on the right and top sides. Place the next photo parallel with the first, using the grid lines as a guide. Use the grid lines to determine the spacing between photos; the photos here are spaced about ¾" apart. Continue this process to place the remaining photos.

3. Print as one sheet

When all photos are placed, go to Layer>Flatten Image. Save your file. Print photos on a sheet of 8½" x 11" (22cm x 28cm) photo paper or cardstock.

4. Cut apart photos

Slide the trimmer blade between two photos. Cut other edges as needed.

Materials

digital photos
Adobe Photoshop Elements
printer
photo paper or cardstock
paper trimmer

[28]

You can tag your layouts with an easy trick.

Tags are so versatile. Use them as journaling spots or as decorative embellishments, or use them on their own as a card for a gift. Or follow my example and use a giant tag as a photo mat for your next layout. Patterned paper can be transformed into a tag to coordinate with any project. But making those perfectly symmetrical corners can be tricky. No worries. With this next tip, you'll be making tags for lots of layouts. Tag, you're it!

Supplies: Cardstock (WorldWin); patterned paper (Making Memories); eyelet (We R Memory Keepers); chipboard letters (American Crafts); Misc: ink

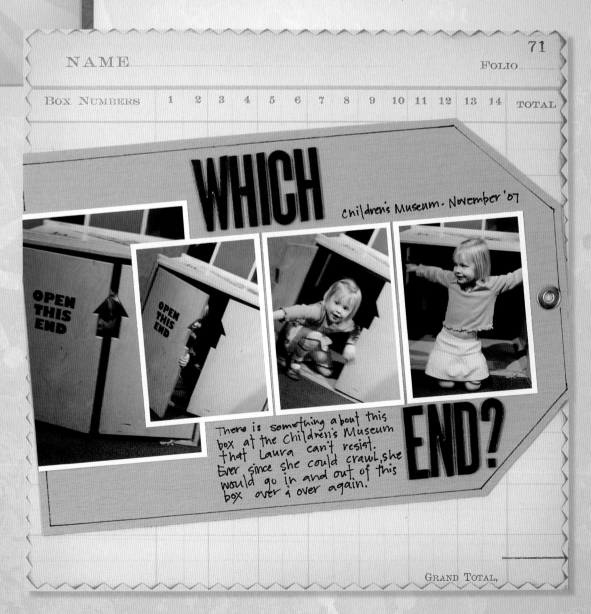

1. Draw line on one corner

Cut a rectangular piece of cardstock to your desired size. Then, using a straightedge as a guide, draw a pencil line at a 45 degree angle on one corner of the rectangular piece. No need to measure or be precise.

2. Cut off corner

Cut off the corner, but don't toss it.

3. Trace triangle

Flip the small triangle over and place it on top of the opposite corner of the rectangle. Trace the edge of the triangle and then cut off that corner.

Materials

cardstock
straightedge
scissors
pencil

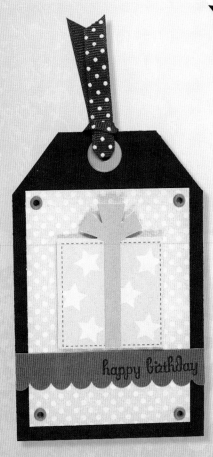

AHA!

It can be tricky to stamp wood-mount stamps in the right spot, especially in narrow spaces like the scalloped border on the tag at left. If you often have trouble, switch to acrylic stamps so you can see exactly where the image will go.

Use this technique to make your own tags for gifts. It's super simple and makes simply adorable tags like this in minutes. Embellish a tag like you would a regular card; stamp a simple sentiment and you're good to go.

Supplies: Cardstock (WorldWin); patterned paper, ribbon (BoBunny); die-cuts (Doodlebug, My Mind's Eye); stamp (Imaginisce); eyelets, paper punch (We R Memory Keepers); Misc: ink

chapter [3]

MakinG Do
SECRETS FOR SCRAPPING IN A PINCH

There are few times when a layout comes together to make the most perfect page without a problem. Usually, being a scrapbooking MacGyver is a necessity, like when you're missing an extra letter A or need a blue star and all you have is green. The good news is that making do doesn't mean layouts that miss the mark. It just means looking at supplies and tools in a different light. And making up for missing embellishments and even fixing a mistake on a layout can often lead to a better page.

1 cute KID

From the day you were born, you have always been

A compass creates perfect rings.

123... **JUMP**

pure energy

I love the look of pure joy as you jump to daddy!

With your fearless nature I knew when daddy asked you to jump you wouldn't hesitate!

Tucson Reid Park Zoo- September 2005

Artwork by Kim Moreno

Circles and rings are great additions to layouts because their round shapes provide movement on a page. Here, Kim uses a large ring to create flow and to mimic the energy of her son. But Kim didn't use a circular template or fancy circle cutter to get that symmetrical shape. She used a tool that we've all used before—in geometry class. A basic compass creates circles and rings at any size you need, even big enough for a 12" (30cm) layout. Grab a compass and you'll be going in circles, too!

Supplies: Cardstock (WorldWin); chipboard accents, eyelets, patterned paper (We R Memory Keepers); rub-ons (American Crafts); cutting machine (Xyron); Misc: ink

AHA!

Go ahead and sketch in pencil on a page. Just keep a white vinyl eraser to clean up any visible pencil marks. A white eraser won't leave the marks on paper that a traditional eraser would.

1. Draw ring's outer edge

Place your paper on a craft mat. Extend the compass to the desired radius (half the width of a circle). Place the pointed end on the paper where you want the middle of the circle to be and hold it in place. Slowly rotate the compass around to make a complete circle. If you want just a circle, stop here and cut it out. (Keep in mind there will be a mark where you placed the compass' pointed end.) To create a ring, move on to Step 2.

2. Draw ring's inner edge

Make the compass' radius $\frac{1}{4}$" (6mm) to $\frac{1}{2}$" (1cm) smaller (depending on your desired ring width). Place the pointed end of the compass back in the same spot on your paper (using the pinpoint as a guide). Again, hold the pointed end in place and slowly rotate the compass around until you make a complete circle.

3. Cut inner circle

Cut out the inside of the paper following along the inner circle. Use micro-tip scissors so it's easy to follow the curve.

4. Cut outer circle

Finish the ring by cutting around the outside circle. Erase any pencil marks as needed.

Everyday dishes can stand in as large circular templates.

–May 2007–

sand surfin'

on the way back from TX we stopped off at White Sands, NM. It was white sand as far as we could see. We had a blast playing in it!!

Artwork by Kim Moreno

Kim added several circles, in both paper and ink, to her layout to mimic the saucer sled her son was using to go sliding on the white sand hills; the largest circle helps ground her photos and pull her whole layout together. Large circles work wonders on a layout. But oftentimes our trusty circle cutters won't make a circle as large as we need to span the width of a layout. It's time to think outside the box—er, circle!—and go beyond your scrap space. Grab a bowl or plate from the kitchen and get the look you want.

Supplies: Cardstock (WorldWin); patterned paper (Arctic Frog); letter stickers (American Crafts); stamps (Fontwerks); brads (Creative Impressions); Misc: floss, ink

1. Trace plate

Chose a plate or other round dish—one that you won't mind running a pencil along. (Now's not the time to break out the fine china you never use!) Lay the dish down on your paper and trace around it with a pencil. Be sure to hold the plate steady so that it doesn't slip during tracing.

2. Cut out circle

Cut out the circle carefully, so that you have nice, even edges. Erase any remaining pencil lines.

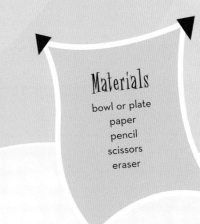

Materials

bowl or plate
paper
pencil
scissors
eraser

AHA!

Make a chipboard template from your dinner plate. Simply trace the plate onto a piece of large chipboard and cut out. It's easier to store the template in your craft space than a dinner plate.

The two of you had so much fun playing in the pool for the week that we visited the Schroeders!

pool pals

Kim added a circle on her layout here, using it as a unique frame for her photo. To mimic Kim's unique technique, cut out a large circle. Then draw a quarter-circle on the inside of the larger shape, about 1/2" (1cm) from its edge. Use a craft knife to cut it out, and then slip your photo right through the slice.

Supplies: Cardstock; letter stickers, patterned paper (American Crafts); Misc: decorative scissors, felt accents, floss

Artwork by Kim Moreno

Circles give
scalloped
borders a
punch.

With its rounded edges, a scalloped border lends a soft and playful look to pages. Whether you've lost your decorative-edge scissors,
you're out of pre-made borders, or want to experiment with something
new, try this clever technique. On my layout here, I used a basic circle
punch to create scallops in a pinch. Tucking circles behind paper to
create the scallops allows you to create a double-colored border like
mine; using a punch provides all kinds of options for size.

Supplies: Cardstock (WorldWin); patterned paper (Anna Griffin); letter stickers (American Crafts);
chipboard shapes (Fancy Pants, Scrapsupply); paper punch (Fiskars); Misc: paint

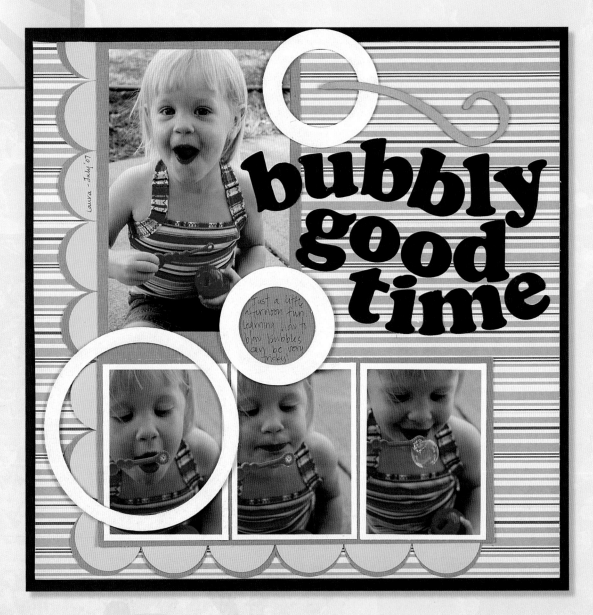

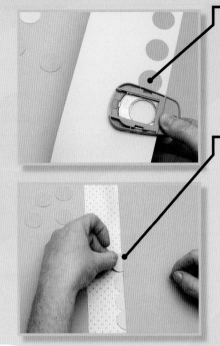

1. Punch circles

Choose a circle punch that fits the scale of your project. For a smaller border with lots of scallops, use a ½" (1cm) punch. Select one sheet of cardstock and punch as many circles as you need to run the length of your border. For a border with two colors, punch the same number of circles out of a second sheet of cardstock in another color.

2. Attach circles to page

Place a strip of paper (like my pink one here) over your background cardstock. Add adhesive to the back of a circle, then slide it halfway under the top piece of paper. Do the same to a second circle, placing it right next to the previous one. Repeat until the border is complete. Add your other set of circles over the top of the first set, allowing some of the first color to peek out.

Materials

cardstock (two colors optional)
circle punch
adhesive
paper

Use scallops to create a fanciful card full of love. Here, Melissa punched out patterned paper circles and dressed them with glitter to create a shining border.

Supplies: Cardstock (WorldWin); patterned paper (BasicGrey, Making Memories); rub-ons (Imaginisce); buttons, sticker (Making Memories); glitter, trim (Melissa Frances); Misc: ink, vintage sheet music

AHA!

With circle punches in multiple sizes, it's easy to lose track of what's what. To keep tabs, label your punches with a permanent marker with the size of the circle.

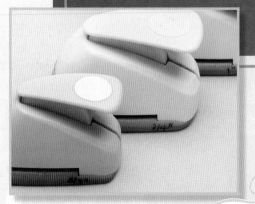

Artwork by Melissa Phillips

[32]

You can work with distracting photos without altering them.

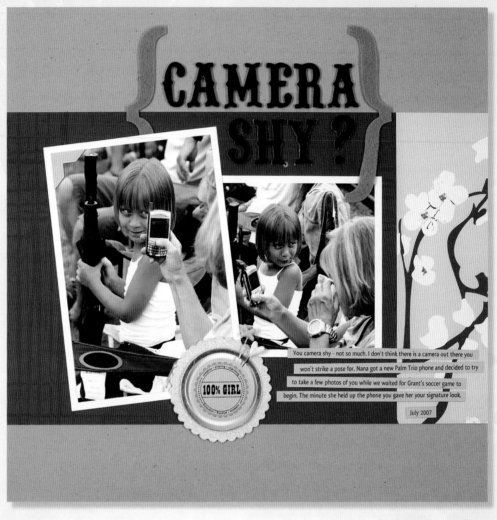

CAMERA SHY?

You camera shy - not so much. I don't think there is a camera out there you won't strike a pose for. Nana got a new Palm Trio phone and decided to try to take a few photos of you while we waited for Grant's soccer game to begin. The minute she held up the phone you gave her your signature look.

July 2007

100% GIRL

Artwork by Summer Fullerton

Sometimes you just love a photo, but it has so many colors it seems impossible to make it work on a page. Often going black-and-white will help, but what about those already-printed pictures, or photos with colors that tell a story? There are ways to make do. Mat photos in black or white (either with a cardstock mat or digital border) to ground them and provide some breathing room between the colors in the photos and the colors in your layout. You can also pull colors from the focal point in your photos and add them to the rest of your page. Summer implemented both of these formulas for success to make her busy photos stand out.

Supplies: Cardstock (WorldWin); felt, patterned paper (Tinkering Ink); chipboard letters (American Crafts); glitter, tag (Making Memories); ribbon (BasicGrey); pins (Fancy Pants); circle punch (Fiskars)

AHA!

Having trouble lining up edges of two patterned papers? Make it easy and attach a strip of one over the other. Then trim all the edges as if it is one sheet.

ADD A PHOTO MAT IN BLACK OR WHITE

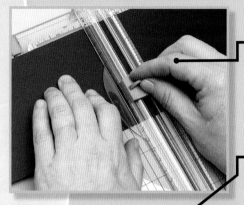

1. Cut cardstock

Using black or white cardstock, cut a rectangle ½" (1cm) wider and higher than your photo. Here's another secret: Cut several rectangles in both black and white to 4½" x 6½" (11cm x 17cm). Then you'll always have a photo mat handy for using with standard-sized photos.

2. Attach photo

Adhere the photo to the mat, eyeballing the placement. The extra ½" (1cm) will equate to a ¼" (6mm) border on all edges of your photo.

Materials

black or white cardstock
paper trimmer
photo
adhesive

PULL OUT IMPORTANT COLORS

1. Choose focal point colors

Survey your photo(s) and choose two or three colors from the focal point of your photo. Here, the girl's white shirt, plus the black umbrella and the red chair framing her are the focal point colors.

2. Include papers in those colors

Choose background papers and main elements in those focal point colors. Here, the red background pulls out the red in the photo. A white photo mat draws the eye straight to the subject. Black title letters also make the subject of the page pop.

Materials

various sheets of patterned paper

Secret

[33]

Journaling errors can be involved in a cover-up.

Every now and then, you're bound to make mistakes when you handwrite journaling. If you're like me, you usually add the journaling at the end of the page-making process, so a mistake can ruin a layout. An easy fix is to cover journaling errors with pieces of cardstock holding the correct word. Cover up a few words and it will actually appear that you meant to highlight certain words for interest. Shhh ... no one will ever know.

Supplies: Cardstock (WorldWin); patterned paper (We R Memory Keepers); chipboard letters (Making Memories); flowers (Imagination Project); rub-ons (BasicGrey); ribbon (May Arts)

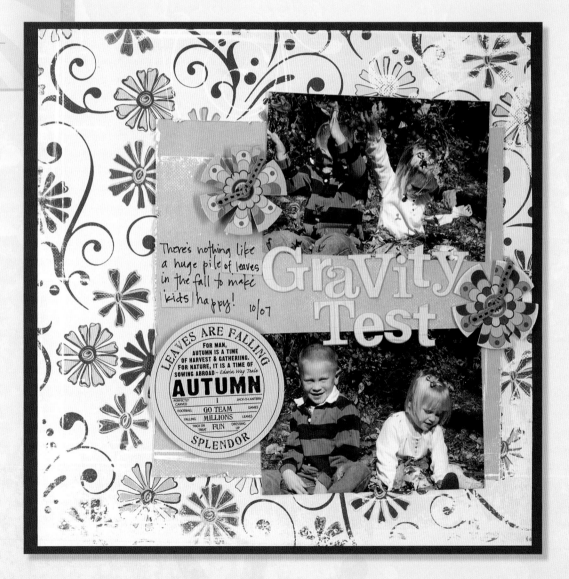

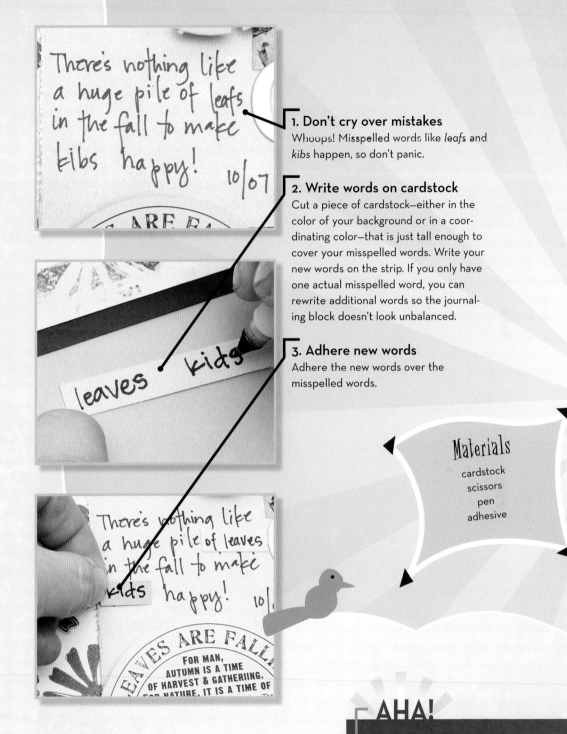

1. Don't cry over mistakes

Whoops! Misspelled words like *leafs* and *kibs* happen, so don't panic.

2. Write words on cardstock

Cut a piece of cardstock—either in the color of your background or in a coordinating color—that is just tall enough to cover your misspelled words. Write your new words on the strip. If you only have one actual misspelled word, you can rewrite additional words so the journaling block doesn't look unbalanced.

3. Adhere new words

Adhere the new words over the misspelled words.

Materials

cardstock
scissors
pen
adhesive

AHA!

Correction tape makes great journaling strips. Just run the tape in lines and write right on the strips of tape with your favorite pen.

Secret

[34]

Hand-cut patterned paper makes great custom embellishments.

Can't find the perfect embellishment? No problem! The perfect accent to match your project is sitting right in front of you—on that sheet of patterned paper. On this layout, Kim cut out the flower accents from patterned paper and added rhinestones and glitter glue to make her own embellishments. These hand-cut accents add unique detail to her layout and, of course, they coordinate since they came from a pattern in the same collection as the other papers she used on her page.

Supplies: Cardstock (WorldWin); chipboard, patterned paper (We R Memory Keepers); rhinestones (Me & My Big Ideas); letter stickers (American Crafts); glitter glue (Ranger)

There is just something about the two of you together, with your big brown eyes. You both just simply sparkle! 4/07

Artwork by Kim Moreno

1. Cut out design
Cut a design out of the piece of patterned paper. Micro-tipped scissors work best for detailed cutting like this; a pair makes it easy to get into all those tight spaces.

2. Add some sparkle
Use glitter glue, rather than messy standard glitter, to add dots of sparkle to your piece.

3. Attach adhesive foam
Use a small piece of adhesive foam to make your embellishment pop on your layout. Place the perfectly matching, brand-new embellishment on your layout.

Materials
patterned paper
micro-tip scissors
glitter glue or rhinestones
adhesive foam

AHA!
For narrow embellishments, cut a piece of the thin strip leftover on a sheet of adhesive foam squares. Or just cut a square in half.

Using adhesive foam isn't the only way to add dimension to hand-cut embellishments. Here, Melissa cut out a few flowers and crinkled them for both texture and dimension. She then layered them over paper in a contrasting color; the crinkles allow the second layer to peek through. Hand-sewn buttons also add dimension to this beautiful card.

Supplies: Cardstock (WorldWin); buttons, patterned paper (Making Memories); letter stickers (EK Success); brads (K&Co.); ribbon (Junkitz); decorative scissors (Fiskars)

Artwork by Melissa Phillips

Artwork by Kim Moreno

Chipboard never fails as an embellishment for adding dimension and flair. Don't you hate it when you encounter the right chipboard shape dressed in the wrong color or (gasp!) not even dressed at all? On this layout, Kim uses ink on her naked chipboard to make it a custom match for her project. Altering dressed or naked chipboard with ink, paint or paper is a great way to make it match your page perfectly. Don't let the fact that a piece doesn't match your layout stop you from using it.

Supplies: Cardstock (WorldWin); patterned paper (CherryArte); chipboard letters and shapes (American Crafts, Magistical Memories); brads (Creative Impressions); photo turn (7gypsies); paper punch (EK Success); Misc: ink

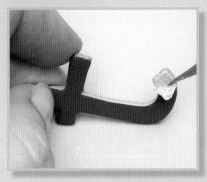

1. (Option A)
Peel away finished surface
If your chipboard is raw, skip to Step 2. If not, use a craft knife to peel back the top, colored layer of the chipboard piece.

1. (Option B)
Sand finished surface
If you prefer, you can use sandpaper to roughen up finished chipboard (so that it will accept paint) and remove the color.

2. (Option A) Paint chipboard
Once chipboard is prepped, add acrylic paint in any color. Apply one thin layer and let it dry before adding a second layer.

2. (Option B) Ink chipboard
Got a great ink color? You can use an ink pad to color chipboard instead of paint. Using chalk ink or pigment ink, simply pat the ink pad along the top of the chipboard until the color saturates the piece.

3. Apply dimensional gloss
To create the glossy look of pre-made colored chipboard, coat the top of the painted (or inked) chipboard piece with dimensional gloss medium. The liquid will be cloudy as you apply it, but it dries clear.

4. Pop air bubbles
Before letting the gloss medium dry, check for air bubbles. Use a thumbtack or paper piercer to pop any air bubbles you find.

AHA!
When painting chipboard, use a cotton swab as a makeshift brush in a pinch.

Materials
chipboard (raw or finished)
craft knife or sandpaper (optional)
paint or ink
paint applicator
dimensional gloss medium
thumbtack or paper piercer

[36]

Shape up! Circles and squares make great substitutes for vowels in a title.

The first letters we run out of on our alpha sheets seem to be the vowels. In the case of my layout below, an a was needed and none were to be found. Fortunately, it's easy to substitute a shape for a vowel in your title. It solves the problem and adds embellishment as well. On my layout, the flower that stands in for my a fits perfectly with the photos of the farmers market.

Supplies: Cardstock (WorldWin); buttons, patterned paper (Making Memories); letter stickers (Reminisce, Rusty Pickle); flower (Petaloo); paper punch (EK Success); Misc: floss

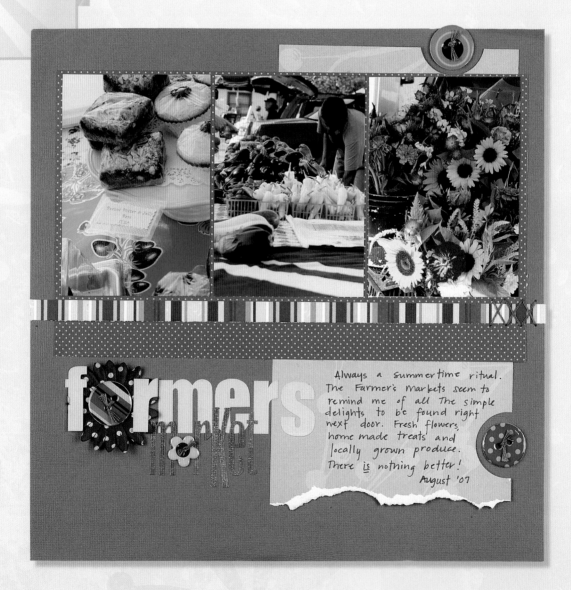

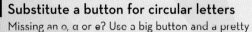

Substitute a button for circular letters

Missing an o, a or e? Use a big button and a pretty ribbon instead. The round shape mimics the missing letter. You can also substitute large brads or round epoxy stickers.

Play up the theme

Look for ways to play up the theme of a word. For example, use a star embellishment in the place of the letter *A* in the word *star*. Or use a chipboard heart in place of the *O* or *V* in *love*.

Use a not-so-obvious shape

The shape you choose doesn't have to match the missing letter. Missing an *a*? Use a flower in its place. It may not resemble an *a* very much, but the word is perfectly clear.

Materials
letters
various shaped embellishments

AHA!

Using adhesive dots is a fast way to attach buttons and other small embellishments to a page. Just place buttons on a row of adhesive dots for quick application.

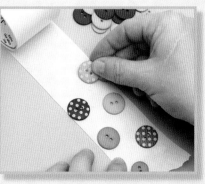

Secret

[37]

You can mix it up to make it work.

Artwork by Kim Moreno

When putting together a long title, most likely you will not have enough of one alpha style to complete it (especially if you're already missing letters). You can quickly and easily solve the dilemma by mixing letters in coordinating sizes and colors. As you can see, the mixed-up title goes perfectly with the silly photos on Kim's layout.

Supplies: Patterned paper (Dream Street); brad, chipboard letters, letter stickers, photo corners, rub-ons (American Crafts); stamp (7gypsies); journaling spot (Heidi Swapp); clip (Li'l Davis); ribbon (Michaels)

AHA!

Tearing paper edges is the quickest way to add dimension and texture to a page.

Mix mismatched letters

Mix it up and use leftover rub-ons, stickers and chipboard alphas to create the title. If you use different styles like these, stick to one hue to make the letters look cohesive. Use letters in similar styles (like those used on Kim's layout on the previous page) when you want to mix colors.

Materials

rub-ons
stickers
chipboard letters

If a layout's eclectic design calls for it, there's no rule against using totally different letters for a title. The playful feel of the crazy, mixed-up title works fantastically for this layout about a family game of Cooties.

Supplies: Cardstock (WorldWin); patterned paper (Cross My Heart, Scenic Route); chipboard letters (Heidi Swapp, Li'l Davis, Pressed Petals, Provo Craft, Scrapworks); sticker (7gypsies); brads (Making Memories); rub-ons (American Crafts)

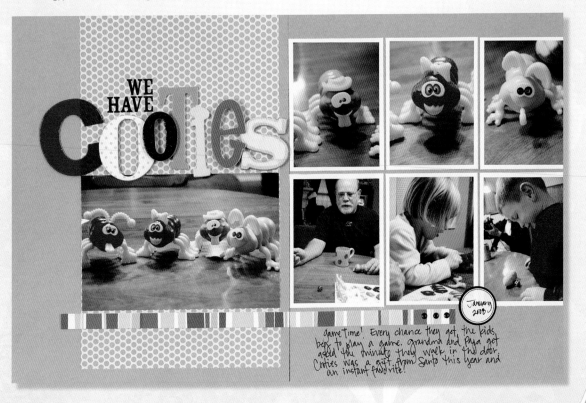

[38]

Cut it out! You can transform extra letter stickers into exactly what you need.

There you are, happily working on your title, when you notice you are short a letter or two. Sound familiar? With so many words and so few letters on a sticker sheet, it's not unusual to find yourself in this situation over and over again. Save this happy moment by transforming another letter, one you actually have in your stash, into the one you need. On this layout, I changed a *d* to an *a* to complete the second *easy* in my title. You'd never know!

Supplies: Cardstock (WorldWin); metal accents, patterned paper, ribbon (We R Memory Keepers); letter stickers (American Crafts, Doodlebug)

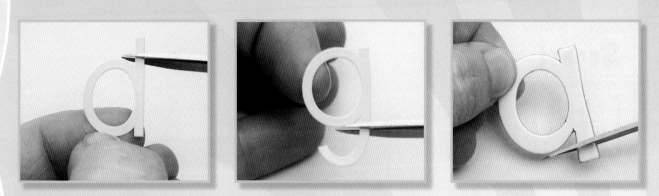

Turn lowercase letters into an a

Snip off the stem of a *d* or *b* or the tail of *p, q* or *g* to make a lowercase *a*. Flip the *b* or *p* to make it work.

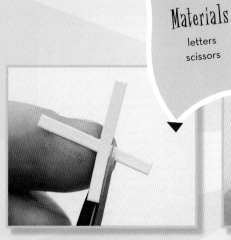

Materials

letters
scissors

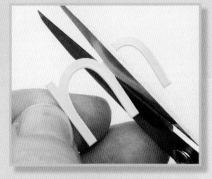

Turn an *m* into an *n* or *u*

To make an *n*, cut off the second curve of the *m*. Flip it upside down to make a *u*.

Turn an *x* into a *y* or *l*

Cut off one of the four parts of the cross to make a *y*. Cut off two parts to make an *l*.

Turn a *j* into an *i*

Cut off the bottom curve of the *j*.

AHA!

Keep white letter stickers on hand. They can be painted or inked to match any project.

chapter [4]

Who Knew?!
SECRETS THAT MAY SURPRISE YOU

Get ready—I'm about to spill some juicy secrets! This chapter is full of tips and tricks that may surprise you. They're the type of techniques that when a friend shared one with me, my mouth hung open and I muttered, "You can do that?" Most of these secrets are things I just had to try for myself; I had to find out if they were really possible! I am still in awe over some of the tricks—but they really work. Who knew?!

U Sparkle

March 2008

You are beyond thrilled with all the 'beautiful' jewelry Aunt 'B' sent for your birthday!

[40]

You can manipulate stamps to get a custom image.

Aaron loves his new space-themed room, from the bedding to the toybox to the "planet" rugs! 4/1/08

There are many benefits to keeping unmounted stamps on hand (hello, easy storage!). One of these is altering them to fit your project needs. For example, a long design or sentiment can be cut to fit a specific area or to say exactly what you want. Yes, it's OK to cut your stamps! Janet cut the sentiment "fly me to the moon" on this layout to create a stacked title to fit the page.

Supplies: Cardstock (WorldWin); patterned paper (Scenic Route); stamps (Inque Boutique); colored pencils (Crayola); digital elements by Katie Pertiet (Designer Digitals); Misc: ink

Artwork by Janet Ohlson

AHA!

CD jewel cases make great storage for unmounted rubber and acrylic stamps.

1. Cut stamp
To make a stacked title, start by cutting the stamp in half.

2. Line up stamp pieces
Place the pieces of stamp along the horizontal lines on a craft mat with a grid (or on lined paper). This will ensure the words in your title are parallel. Place the acrylic block over the stamps.

3. Stamp image
Ink the stamp and stamp the image. Be careful not to rock the stamp and create smudges.

Materials
unmounted stamp
sharp scissors
craft mat with grid lines or lined paper
acrylic stamp block
ink pad

Cutting long stamp phrases works especially well for the small surface area on greeting cards. Kim clipped her stamp and stacked the words to help them fit this beautiful card. Cutting stamps also allows you to select just a few words from a phrase.

Cardstock (WorldWin); patterned paper (7gypsies); ribbon (Beaux Regards); pin (Fancy Pants); stamps (Cornish Heritage Farms, Daisy Bucket); distress tool (Tim Holtz); Misc: beads, ink

Artwork by Kim Hughes

Secret

[41]

Stamps make great stencils for hand-cut embellishments.

If you read Chapter 3, you know that hand-cutting patterned paper makes great coordinating embellishments for a layout. But what do you do when your pattern doesn't have the right detail—or any detail at all? Look at your stamps in a whole new light! Stamping on the back of a piece of patterned paper and cutting out the shape will give you a fabulous accent for your page, like these trees that dress up my layout here. What's more, if you're not such a great stamper, you've got a whole new way to use those tools.

Supplies: Cardstock (WorldWin); patterned paper (BasicGrey, Fontwerks); die-cuts (Doodlebug); letter stickers (BasicGrey); stamps (Super T's); brads (Creative Impressions, Making Memories); Misc: corner rounder

DECK the HaLLS

good old Christmas time! I do enjoy the decoration of the house but part way through the process, my enthusiasm wanes a bit. The kid's excitement tends to help push me along. when it's all done, I love the end result.

december 2007

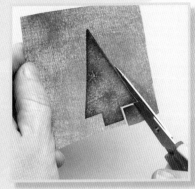

1. Stamp image
Stamp your image on the reverse side of the patterned paper.

2. Cut out stamped image
Cut out the stamped image with micro-tip scissors.

3. Mat shape with cardstock
To make your embellishment stand out on your page, adhere the cut-out image onto a piece of coordinating cardstock. Trim around the edges, leaving a small border. Alternatively, you can ink the edges. You can also add adhesive foam to make the embellishment pop.

Materials

patterned paper
rubber or acrylic stamp
ink pad
micro-tip scissors
adhesive
cardstock
(optional) adhesive foam

AHA!

Most solvent ink pads come with a plastic cover to help keep the pad moist. To keep that plastic piece from jumping around or getting lost, place an adhesive dot on top then close it back up. The adhesive dot will stick to the inside of the main lid.

Secret

[42]

Busy photo backgrounds can disappear like magic.

thankful *that you love to bake, because I don't! Pumpkin chocolate tart, baked November 2003*

BAKER

Artwork by Vivian Masket

Vivian wanted to document her husband, the baker of the family, on a layout. She had this photo for a few years and was stumped on how to scrap it due to its rather distracting background. She solved the problem by brushing acrylic paint over the background in the photo. Brilliant! Follow Vivian's lead and use the same color paint as your cardstock, and presto!—watch as the photo blends into the layout. This trick also works to highlight your subject.

Supplies: Cardstock (WorldWin); patterned paper (KI Memories); transparency (Hambly); chipboard letters (Heidi Swapp); felt (Fancy Pants); stamp (Autumn Leaves); Misc: circle cutter, ink, paint

Brush paint over photo

Attach the photo to the background cardstock. Brush paint over the background of the photo and cover up any unwanted details. Extend the paint onto the cardstock for a seamless transition.

Materials

photo

cardstock

adhesive

acrylic paint
(same color as cardstock)

paintbrush

AHA!

You can blur distracting backgrounds using Photoshop. Just click on the lasso tool, outline your background and go to Filter>Blur>Gaussian blur.

IT'S HARD

TO BE 3

4/08

It's so rough when you can't always get your own way. At 3, your not quite sure how to express your frustrations yet.

After seeing Vivian's idea for masking the background of a photo, I knew exactly how I wanted to scrap this photo of my daughter having a little temper tantrum. The jagged way I brushed the paint over the photo matches the anger my daughter was trying to express. The paint covers up the busy background that adds nothing to the story of the photo.

Supplies: Cardstock (WorldWin); die-cut cardstock (KI Memories); chipboard letters (American Crafts); Misc: paint

[43]

You can split a photo over the seam of a two-page layout.

Two-page layouts are great for those times when you need a large canvas to work with. But the seam presents a roadblock when you want to center a photo on the layout. Well, it doesn't need to be! As Summer's layout shows, cardstock, titles and, yes, even photos can be successfully split along the seam. In fact, placing a photo on both halves of a spread unifies the design. Just remember to avoid splitting a photo over a subject's face, and you're good to go.

Supplies: Cardstock (WorldWin); patterned paper (Tinkering Ink); chipboard (Heidi Swapp); eyelets (Making Memories); metal clips (Provo Craft); label (Dymo); die-cutter (Xyron)

Artwork by Summer Fullerton

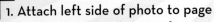
1. Attach left side of photo to page
Place your photo over the seam of a two-page layout. Make sure the seam will run through the background of the photo and not through a subject's face. Adhere only the part of the photo on the left-hand page of the layout.

2. Cut off right side of photo
Flip the background paper over and carefully trim off the strip of photo that hangs off the paper. Save the cut-off strip.

3. Attach right side of photo
Place both background pages of the layout together. Adhere the strip of photo to the right page of the layout, carefully lining up both sides of the photo.

Materials
cardstock (two sheets)
photo
adhesive
paper trimmer

AHA!
Break into your stash of office supplies to add quick and creative text to your layout. Summer used a Dymo labeler to add the date to her layout (left; detail at right). A labeler is also great for adding photo captions, for mini albums and for including fun details on cards.

APRIL 2005

[44]

You can have more fun with flowers.

If you're like me, you have tons of flowers in your stash. Adding a single button or brad in the center of them can get a little tiresome. Summer mixed it up a bit by adding glittered brads layered over punched circles in the centers of her flowers. (Did you know you can actually use the leftover holes created with a standard hole punch?) Just that little bit of ingenuity adds a lot of visual interest to her layout. You can get the same look with your own stash of brads and a hole punch. Take some time to stop and smell the flowers and have a little fun.

Supplies: Cardstock (WorldWin); patterned paper (Tinkering Ink); felt flowers (American Crafts); brads (Doodlebug); Misc: floss

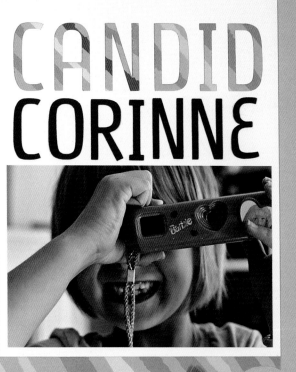

Today was the first/second grade rummage sale at school. It's a simple and fun activity designed to teach the children about money. The first graders are given play money and the second graders bring in items from home they wish to sell. Turns out you are quite the little shopper and you came home with a whole bag full of goodies. Your prime purchase of the day was this Barbie camera. You ran around the house *click click click* "say cheese." It was my turn to be on the other side of the camera but how could I resist not snapping my own photo of my little candid Corinne. 1rst Grade 5/07

CANDID CORINNE

Artwork by Summer Fullerton

108

1. Punch circles

Punch out circles in the paper with the hole punch.

2. Insert brad in circle

Pierce a hole in the center of each circle with a thumbtack or paper piercer. Push the brad through the hole in the circle. Be careful not to bend or crush your tiny circle.

3. Insert brad in flower

Pierce a hole in the flower with the thumbtack or paper piercer. Push the brad/circle through the flower and open the brad's prongs to set it. Cluster several brads/circles to fill the center of a larger flower.

Materials

1/4" (6mm) hole punch
paper
thumbtack or paper piercer
brads
silk or paper flower

AHA!

If a punch starts to dull, punch through sandpaper or aluminum foil to sharpen the blade.

Anja adds a funky twist to the center of her flower using multi-colored sequins. The look fits the fun and silliness of her photos. With pre-punched holes, sequins are great for dressing up brads. But they're an unexpected element that look fabulous on their own as Anja's layout illustrates.

Supplies: Cardstock (WorldWin); flower (Petaloo); Misc: floss, sequins

Artwork by Anja Wade

Secret

[45]

Brads can be embellished.

A large brad is a nice, bold accent for a page. A large brad all dressed up is even better! If you're bored with brads, you can alter them to suit your heart's desires. You can change any brad with rub-ons, ink or embossing powder to embellish a layout. Who knew? Apparently Kim knew the secret because on this page, she used large, plain brads transformed with floral rub-ons to take her design from good to wow.

friends

I love the friendship the two of you have developed over the years. Chris and I have been best friends for over 12 years and it's neat to see the two of you carrying that on. You may only see each other a few times a year, but each time you two pick up where you left off. Both of you are SO much alike in your mannerisms, in your behavoirs, and your interests. I hope that this friendship will only continue to grow stronger over the years. Madison and Hannah·August 2005

Supplies: Cardstock (WorldWin); patterned paper (Glitz Design); rhinestones (Westrim); flowers (Petaloo); brads (American Crafts, Bazzill); rub-ons (Polar Bear Press); dimensional adhesive (JudiKins); die-cutting machine (Xyron)

Artwork by Kim Moreno

Materials
large brad
rub-on image

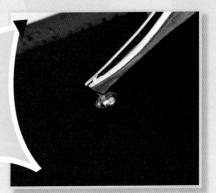

Materials
large brad
solvent ink
tweezers

ADD A RUB-ON

Apply rub-on and trim excess

Flat brads are the easiest to work with, but you can use curved brads as well. Apply the rub-on to the top of the large brad. Trim any part of the rub-on that hangs off the edges.

INK A BRAD

Dip brad in ink

To color the top of the brad, hold it with tweezers and press it into a solvent ink pad. The solvent ink will stick to the slick surface and dry quickly.

EMBOSS A BRAD

1. Heat brad

Hold the brad with tweezers. (You don't want to burn your fingers!) Apply heat from the heat gun to the brad, just long enough to heat it.

2. Dip brad in powder

Dip the hot brad into a shallow container filled with extra thick embossing powder. Make sure the brad is covered with powder.

3. Melt embossing powder

Reheat the brad with the heat gun until the powder melts completely. The powder will coat the brad's surface with a shiny coat of color.

Materials
brad in any size
tweezers
extra thick embossing powder
heat gun

AHA!

To make embossing powder or glitter clean-up quick, place a piece of paper under your project to collect extra powder. Then place a funnel over a jar with a small opening to ensure all the powder gets back in.

[46]

You can use the color "bleed" left over on a sheet of used-up stickers.

Stretching your supplies to the very end is a smart way to get the most out of them. It also allows for creative elements that make a page stand out against the rest. Here, Kim trimmed the edge of a sticker S that was left on a sheet of letters after use. Many times you have to be a little creative to make the title you want work, but layouts are often better for it.

Supplies: Cardstock (WorldWin); patterned paper (Dream Street); brads (Bazzill, Doodlebug); journaling spot (Jenni Bowlin); metal clip (Li'l Davis); stickers (Adornit, Cloud 9, Doodlebug, SEI); felt (Queen & Co.); paper trimmer (Creative Memories)

memories

Makenna & I kept ourselves entertained by snapping photos on the bus. Kinder field trip to the Pumpkin patch '07

snapshots from the BUS

Artwork by Kim Moreno

1. Cut out sticker bleed

Cut around the sticker color "bleed" left on the sheet of stickers. Using the micro-tip scissors will allow you to get in the tight spaces between letters. Be careful to cut right along the edge of the color.

2. Trim edges

Trim any white edges that are left after the letter is cut out entirely. Now admire your cool outline letter!

Materials

letter sticker sheet
micro-tip scissors

AHA!

Forgot to save your sticker leftovers? When all else fails, just use stamps. To save money, invest in generic words you'll use over and over again, like *birthday*, *fun* and *party*. Or better yet, just buy individual letter stamps.

Supplies: Cardstock (WorldWin); brads, patterned paper (Making Memories); chipboard accents (Cosmo Cricket); Misc: ink, stamp

[47]

A circle can help you do the wave.

A giant wave creates motion and moves the reader's eye across the page. Kim's wave below directs the eye from the upper corner of the layout through her photos and down to her journaling. How'd she get that perfectly symmetrical wave? She discovered that using two circles, or in her case two rings, and joining them up under a pattern paper strip will create the perfect wave. What a great idea!

Supplies: Cardstock (WorldWin); patterned paper (My Mind's Eye); chipboard (Magistical Memories); letter stickers (Doodlebug, Scenic Route); brads (American Crafts, Bazzill); decorative scissors (Fiskars); Misc: ink

Artwork by Kim Moreno

AHA!

Place a small eraser on the sharp tip of your compass to keep it from poking a hole in your paper.

1. Draw large circle

Draw a circle on the sheet of paper or cardstock. The radius (half the width) of the circle will be the height of the wave. If you want your wave to be just a line, then draw a ring.

2. Cut out circle

Cut out the circle (or ring) with scissors. Erase any pencil marks as needed.

3. Cut circle in half

Cut your circle in half. I use my trimmer to make sure the cut is straight and is in the center of the circle.

4. Match up corners

Place your circle halves on your background so that the corner of one meets the corner of the other. One half-circle should be placed with the curve at the bottom and one should have the curve at the top. It's OK if the circles hang off the edge of the layout.

5. Trim edges of half-circles

Flip over the background and trim off any part of the half-circles that hang over the edge of the layout.

6. Cut paper strip

Cut a thin strip of paper the length of the wave. Adhere it over the middle of the wave to disguise the edges of the half-circles.

Materials

cardstock or paper
compass (optional)
pencil
scissors
paper trimmer (optional)
adhesive

[48]

A trimmer and stylus score one for your layout.

Using the scoring blade on your trimmer can be tricky; half the time the blade is lost, and the other half you push so hard you tear a hole in your cardstock. (Grrr ...) The good news is you can use a stylus with your trimmer in place of the scoring blade to create the perfect score line. There's more good news: Scoring lines isn't just for creating folds in a cards. I created the basket weave on this layout with score lines. Rubbing chalk ink over the raised, scored lines brings out the texture of the scoring.

Supplies: Cardstock (WorldWin); patterned paper (Making Memories, Scenic Route); letter stickers (American Crafts); flowers, ribbon (Making Memories); die-cuts (Doodlebug); brads (Creative Impressions, Doodlebug); paper trimmer (Fiskars); Misc: ink

In the wee hours of the morning the Easter Bunny makes a delivery of a basket full of goodies!

~easter '08~

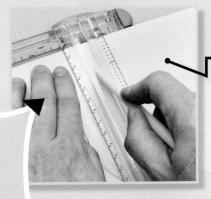

SCORE A FOLD

Score down center

Score a line down the center of the card. Use the blade rail (the part where the blade slides) on the trimmer to run the stylus's point down the paper.

Materials

cardstock
paper trimmer
stylus
chalk ink or sandpaper

SCORE A BASKET WEAVE

1. Begin scoring

Use the stylus and trimmer to score a line every ½" (1cm) down one side of the cardstock.

2. Turn paper and finish scoring

Rotate the cardstock 90 degrees to the right. Score every ½" (1cm) again down the cardstock. If your paper is a light color, rub chalk over the paper to make the texture stand out. You can also use a sanding tool for the same effect.

AHA!

You can substitute a basic emery board for a sanding tool or sponge.

Kim added texture and a subtle design element to this card by adding a few score lines in the middle. Of course, the folds in the cards are created with score lines, too.

Artwork by Kim Hughes

Supplies: Cardstock (WorldWin); patterned paper (Creative Imaginations); chipboard letters (Making Memories); scoring tool (EK Success); Misc: paint

[49]

**Just one sheet
of paper can
make
four large
photo mats.**

Can you get four 5" x 7" (13cm x 18cm) photo mats out of just one sheet of 12" x 12" (30cm x 30cm) paper? Marci's layout shows you can. I had no idea! I was cutting papers for a class when Marci grabbed my trimmer and a sheet of paper and taught me this trick. Matting photos in neutral-colored cardstock is a no-fail way to make photos pop, but it's also a way to eat up paper fast. So try out this trick to make the most of your cardstock ... and amaze your friends!

Supplies: Cardstock (WorldWin); patterned paper (BasicGrey, Prima); journaling spot, letter stickers (Making Memories); flowers (Prima); rhinestones (Heidi Swapp); ribbon (Michaels); Misc: floss

Artwork by Marci Lambert

AHA!

To make a quick photo corner, punch a square and then cut it at a diagonal to create two triangles.

1. Set paper in trimmer
Line up the cardstock on the 5" (13cm) mark on your trimmer's arm.

2. Make first cut
Cut the cardstock down to the 7" (18cm) mark on the blade rail.

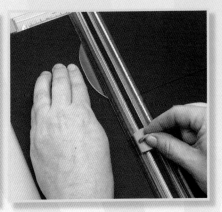

3. Rotate and cut
Rotate the cardstock 90 degrees to the right. Place edge of the cardstock on the 5" (13cm) mark of your trimmer and cut down to the 7" (18cm) mark again.

4. Rotate and make third cut
Rotate the cardstock 90 degrees again to the right. Place the edge of the cardstock on the 5" (13cm) mark on your trimmer and cut down to the 7" (18cm) mark.

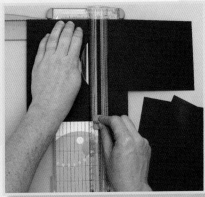

5. Rotate and make final cut
Rotate the cardstock one last time 90 degrees to the right. Line up the paper on the 5" (13cm) mark on your trimmer and cut down to the 7" (18cm) mark.

6. Check your work
When you're finished, check that you have four 5" x 7" (13cm x 18cm) pieces of cardstock and one 1" square piece.

Materials
12" (30cm) sheet of cardstock
paper trimmer

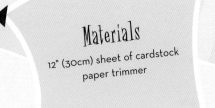

[50]

You can use a corner rounder to create a scalloped-edge border.

It's no secret by now that scalloped edges are a great way to soften the lines on a layout or card. They add texture and depth in a subtle way. There are many materials on the market for adding scallops, like decorative scissors and trimmer blades and pre-made scalloped strips. Here's the real secret: You can use a tool you already have in your scrapper's took kit to make a scallop border. On this layout, I used a basic corner rounder to punch scalloped edges on my pastel patterned paper. Pre-made versus handmade: Can you even tell the difference?

Supplies: Chipboard accents, letter stickers, patterned paper, ribbon (Making Memories); tag (Martha Stewart); pin (Heidi Grace); corner rounder (EK Success)

AHA!

You can round corners of chipboard pieces with cool new tools by Zutter and Around the Block.

1. Remove plastic guard
If your corner rounder has a plastic guard, remove it before punching.

2. Make first punch
Turn the punch over so you can see where you are punching. To make your first scallop, place the "corner" part of the punch along the edge of your paper. Place one end of the rounded part of the punch at the corner of your paper.

3. Finishing punching
Carefully line up the punch with the first scallop punched. Again, place the corner part of the punch along the edge of your paper. Place the same end of the rounded part of the punch at the end of the first scallop. There should be a little space on the edge in the punch window. Continue punching until your scalloped edge is complete.

Variation
You can use this technique to create a scalloped circle or curve. Just draw a curve or circle in pencil to guide your punching. Line up the scallops as you would on a straight line.

Materials
corner rounder
paper
(optional) pencil

Contributors

The talented team of contributors shares their own secrets!

KIM MORENO Tucson, Arizona

Kim Moreno was born and raised in Texas. She married young to a military man, Jesse, and has since lived in several places. She is currently stationed in Tucson, Arizona, but looks forward to retirement very soon and heading back to the family's lakefront property in Texas. Kim is the proud mom of five little ones ranging in age from 12 to six-year-old twins. Life is a bit crazy, but loads of fun!

Kim has been scrapbooking since 2000. She has since designed for several manufacturers and has been published in a variety of magazines including *Creating Keepsakes, Memory Makers, BHG Scrapbooks. Etc., Scrapbook Trends, Cards, Paper Crafts* and more. Kim is also 2008 Memory Makers Master Runner Up.

Kim enjoys knowing she is documenting memories for her children to look back on and enjoy when they are older.

"We all tend to make mistakes when creating our layouts (well, I do at least), but there's no need to toss it! I think every mistake can be covered, rearranged or hidden, and no one will be the wiser. That's the reason I love this book; there are so many ideas to do just that!"

SUMMER FULLERTON Tigard, Oregon

Summer's creative journey began at a young age. She grew up surrounded by inspiration: Her mother made dolls, jewelry, pottery and even designed wallpaper. It seemed natural for Summer to take a creative path in life as well. She received her first camera in 1976, and although it wasn't loaded with film until many years later, the seeds of artistry had been planted.

After the birth of her first child, Summer discovered scrapbooking as we know it today and has been hooked ever since. In 2007, she was named to the Creating Keepsakes Hall of Fame, and she is a 2009 Memory Makers Master. Her published creations can be seen in *Creating Keepsakes, Scrapbooks Etc., Simple Scrapbooks, Paper Trends, Scrapbook Trends, Paper Crafts* and *Cards* and *Memory Makers.*

Summer lives with her husband of 14 years, Brad, and her 2 children, Grant and Corinne, in Oregon.

"Sometimes I find that a layout needs one final touch to bring everything together. Right now that touch is the little black line. The simple black line often grounds my work giving it just the right amout of interest without overwhelming the page.

Contributors

YVONNE BUSDEKER Woodridge, Illinois

"I'm addicted to Tinkering Ink's greaseless lotion (unscented) because I can use it for crafting. I have a large bottle in my office and a smaller bottle that travels bag to bag. I'm never without it. I could be a poster child for this awesome stuff!"

LISA DORSEY Westfield, Indiana

"A page doesn't feel complete to me if I don't include at least one piece of patterned paper. I usually have more. To make sure the papers don't clash I try to vary the sizes of the print or break them up with a solid color."

PAULA GILARDE Bedford, Massachusetts

"You don't have to scrap everything right away. Sometimes it's good to save some photos for later when you want to re-live a memory."

LINDA HARRISON Sarasota, Florida

"Looking back through my albums, my favorite pages seem to be the ones with the fewest embellishments. I don't know if it is because the story and the photos remain the stars of the show, or if it is just the look I like. But it has taught me that a single, well-placed embellishment makes a bigger impact than 10 of something that have nothing to do with my page."

SARAH HODGKINSON Woodstock, Ontario, Canada

"My scrapbooking secret is a bit bizarre. I love the smell of Jet Black StazOn ink by Tsukineko. Give it a sniff and you'll see what I mean. Just don't get it on the end of your nose. They really mean 'StazOn'!"

KIM HUGHES Roy, Utah

"I use dried baby wipes to rub off excess dust from sanding. It's gentle on the paper and doesn't tear it up."

MARCI LAMBERT Memphis, Tennessee

"I sort all my embellishments by color in canvas bins. When I finish a project, I literally just toss stuff right back into the bins. It's very easy and quick to clean up!"

VIVIAN MASKET Denver, Colorado

"I create a two-photo collage on 4" x 6" (10cm x 15cm) photo paper to both save on printing costs and easily get multiple photos onto my layouts (especially 8½" x 11" [22cm x 28cm] layouts)."

JANET OHLSON Plainfield, Illinois

"My secret is that there is nothing in life that can't be laughed at."

MELISSA PHILLIPS Caliente, Nevada

"I love to bring my cards to life by forgetting about the space I am given to create on and forgetting about how it will possibly fit into the envelope. I love to add in puffy bows, dimensional elements such as buttons, tags, wrapped string and flowers in order to make the card something that someone might possibly want to touch and run their fingers across and then keep forever."

JANELLE RICHMOND Kingsland, Georgia

"Always keep a basket of your favorite photos on your desk, so you can be inspired by them. It helps keep the mojo flowin'."

KATRINA SIMECK Colchester, Vermont

"Cleanliness is next to scrappiness! I absolutely have to clean up my scrap table before I can start a new project. If I don't start with a clean slate, nothing flows well."

SHERRY STEVESON Wilmington, North Carolina

"I lay all my photos down on paper, figure out where I want to place them and then use glue dots under the corners. I do this instead of lifting up each photo and applying double sided tape and trying to figure out where I originally positioned them."

ANJA WADE Warren, Massachusetts

"My scrap secret is that I usually like messy, hand-written block letter titles better than fancy store-bought letters. And sometimes I staple things down out of sheer laziness."

Source Guide

The following companies manufacture products featured in this book. Please check your local retailers to find these materials, or go to a company's Web site for the latest product. In addition, we have made every attempt to properly credit the items mentioned in this book. We apologize to any company that we have listed incorrectly, and we would appreciate hearing from you. Special thanks to Fiskars and WorldWin Papers for generously donating products toward the creation of artwork in this book.

7gypsies
(877) 749-7797
www.sevengypsies.com

Adornit/Carolee's Creations
(435) 563-1100
www.adornit.com

American Crafts
(801) 226-0747
www.americancrafts.com

Anna Griffin, Inc.
(888) 817-8170
www.annagriffin.com

Arctic Frog
www.arcticfrog.com

Around The Block
(801) 593-1946
www.aroundtheblock
products.com

Autumn Leaves
(800) 588-6707
www.autumnleaves.com

BasicGrey
(801) 544-1116
www.basicgrey.com

Bazzill Basics Paper
(480) 558-8557
www.bazzillbasics.com

Beaux Regards
(203) 438-1105
www.beauxregards.com

BoBunny Press
(801) 771-4010
www.bobunny.com

CherryArte
(212) 465-3495
www.cherryarte.com

Cloud 9 Design
(866) 348-5661
www.cloud9design.biz

Cornish Heritage Farms
(877) 860-5328
www.cornishheritagefarms.com

Cosmo Cricket
(800) 852-8810
www.cosmocricket.com

Crate Paper
(801) 798-8996
www.cratepaper.com

Crayola
(800) 272-9652
www.crayola.com

Creative Imaginations
(800) 942-6487
www.cigift.com

Creative Impressions
(719) 596-4860
www.creativeimpressions.com

Creative Memories
(800) 468-9335
www.creativememories.com

Cross-My-Heart-Cards, Inc.
(888) 689-8808
www.crossmyheart.com

Daisy Bucket Designs
(541) 289-3299
www.daisybucketdesigns.com

Daisy D's Paper Company
(888) 601-8955
www.daisydspaper.com

Designer Digitals
www.designerdigitals.com

DMC Corp.
(973) 589-0606
www.dmc-usa.com

Doodlebug Design Inc.
(877) 800-9190
www.doodlebug.ws

Dream Street Papers
(480) 275-9736
www.dreamstreetpapers.com

Dymo
(800) 426-7827
www.dymo.com

EK Success, Ltd.
www.eksuccess.com

Fancy Pants Designs, LLC
(801) 779-3212
www.fancypantsdesigns.com

Fiskars, Inc.
(866) 348-5661
www.fiskars.com

Fontwerks
(604) 942-3105
www.fontwerks.com

Glitz Design
(866) 356-6131
www.glitzitnow.com

Hambly Screenprints
(800) 707-0977
www.hamblyscreenprints.com

Hampton Art Stamps, Inc.
(800) 229-1019
www.hamptonart.com

Heidi Grace Designs, Inc.
(866) 347-5277
www.heidigrace.com

Heidi Swapp/Advantus Corporation
(904) 482-0092
www.heidiswapp.com

Hero Arts Rubber Stamps, Inc.
(800) 822-4376
www.heroarts.com

Imagination Project, Inc.
(888) 477-6532
www.imaginationproject.com

Imaginisce
(801) 908-8111
www.imaginisce.com

Inkadinkado Rubber Stamps
(800) 523-8452
www.inkadinkado.com

Inque Boutique Inc.
www.inqueboutique.com

Jenni Bowlin
www.jennibowlin.com

JudiKins
(310) 515-1115
www.judikins.com

Junkitz
(732) 792-1108
www.junkitz.com

K&Company
(888) 244-2083
www.kandcompany.com

Karen Foster Design
(801) 451-9779
www.karenfosterdesign.com

KI Memories
(972) 243-5595
www.kimemories.com

Li'l Davis Designs
(480) 223-0080
www.lildavisdesigns.com

Magistical Memories
(818) 842-1540
www.magisticalmemories.com

Making Memories
(801) 294-0430
www.makingmemories.com

Martha Stewart Crafts
www.marthastewartcrafts.com

May Arts
(800) 442-3950
www.mayarts.com

Maya Road, LLC
(877) 427-7764
www.mayaroad.com

Me & My Big Ideas
(949) 583-2065
www.meandmybigideas.com

Melissa Frances/Heart & Home, Inc.
(888) 616-6166
www.melissafrances.com

Memories Complete, LLC
(866) 966-6365
www.memoriescomplete.com

Michaels Arts & Crafts
www.michaels.com

My Mind's Eye, Inc.
(800) 665-5116
www.mymindseye.com

Paper Trunk
(503) 855-3323
www.papertrunk.com

Pebbles Inc.
(801) 235-1520
www.pebblesinc.com

Petaloo
www.petaloo.com

Pink Paislee
(816) 729-6124
www.pinkpaislee.com

Polar Bear Press
(801) 451-7670
www.polarbearpress.com

Pressed Petals
(801) 224-6766
www.pressedpetals.com

Prima Marketing, Inc.
(909) 627-5532
www.primamarketinginc.com

Provo Craft
(800) 937-7686
www.provocraft.com

Queen & Co.
(858) 613-7858
www.queenandcompany.com

Ranger Industries, Inc.
(800) 244-2211
www.rangerink.com

Reminisce Papers
(319) 358-9777
www.shopreminisce.com

Rusty Pickle
(801) 746-1045
www.rustypickle.com

Sandylion Sticker Designs
(800) 387-4215
www.sandylion.com

Sassafras Lass
(801) 269-1331
www.sassafraslass.com

Scenic Route Paper Co.
(801) 542-8071
www.scenicroutepaper.com

Scrapsupply
(615) 777-3953
www.scrapsupply.com

Scrapworks, LLC
(801) 363-1010
www.scrapworks.com

SEI, Inc.
(800) 333-3279
www.shopsei.com

Stampin' Up!
(800) 782-6787
www.stampinup.com

Super T's LLC
(435) 864-3778
www.super-ts.com

Tim Holtz
www.timholtz.com

Time Flies Design
(845) 726-3646
www.timefliesdesign.net

Tinkering Ink
(877) 727-2784
www.tinkeringink.com

Urban Lily
www.urbanlily.com

We R Memory Keepers, Inc.
(801) 539-5000
www.weronthenet.com

Webster's Pages/
Webster Fine Art Limited
(800) 543-6104
www.websterspages.com

Westrim Crafts
(800) 727-2727
www.westrimcrafts.com

WorldWin Papers
(888) 834-6455
www.worldwinpapers.com

Xyron
(800) 793-3523
www.xyron.com

Index

The two of you had so much fun playing in the pool for the week that we visited the Schroeders!

For more tips and ideas, check out these other Memory Makers Books.

See what's coming up from Memory Makers Books by checking out our blogs:
www.mycraftivity.com/scrapbooking_papercrafts/blog/
www.memorymakersmagazine.com/blog/

Making the Most of Your Scrapbook Supplies

Innovative ideas from the Memory Makers Masters for using that growing stash of scrapbook supplies and tools.
ISBN-13: 978-1-59963-012-0
ISBN-10: 1-59963-012-5
paperback
128 pages
Z1040

The Busy Scrapper

You can scrap fast and hassle-free! Packed with tips and techniques showing you how to scrap in a flash, this book is a one-stop guide to efficient layouts that are fun to make.
ISBN-13: 978-1-59963-029-8
ISBN-10: 1-59963-029-X
paperback
128 pages
Z2141

Scrap Simple

Scrapbooking doesn't have to be fussy to be fun! *Scrap Simple* makes it easy to whip up clean and uncluttered scrapbook pages in a flash.
ISBN-13: 978-1-59963-014-4
ISBN-10: 1-59963-014-1
paperback
128 pages
Z1282

These books and other Memory Makers titles are available at your local scrapbook retailer, bookstore or from online suppliers, or visit our Web sites at www.memorymakersmagazine.com or www.mycraftivity.com.